ENTERTAINING CHILDREN

*This book is dedicated to my family—
my husband David, my daughter Julie,
my son Chris, my daughter-in-law Kim,
my granddaughter Sarah, and my grandson Bryan*

ENTERTAINING CHILDREN

Theme Parties, Activities, Games and Fun Ideas for Groups

by
JANELL SHRIDE AMOS

McFarland & Company, Inc., Publishers
Jefferson, North Carolina, and London

Drawings by Ronald C. Kilkenney; photos by Christopher D. Amos

Acknowledgments: With gratitude I acknowledge the contributions of the family members and friends who helped with the preparation of this book.

My grandchildren, Sarah and Bryan, were ever willing to take part in my activities, play my games and spend hours with the camera recording their fun. My son Chris took photographs used to illustrate the book and was generous with his advice and encouragement. His wife Kim helped with the photo sessions, critiqued my manuscript, and served as my crafts consultant. My daughter Julie helped make sample decorated cakes and craft projects. My husband David proofread the manuscript and, most important of all, was accepting of the many hours I devoted to this project. It was indeed a family affair.

The children in the photographs are Bryan Amos, Sarah Amos, Stephanie Bean, Lindsay Bliggenstorfer, Lauren Browne, Timothy Browne, Meghan Carter, Nicholas Carter, J. P. Davis, Allison Fenster, Joshua Fenster, Christopher Flahan, Paul Flahan, Kelly Freeze, Michael Freeze, Kelly Janik, Kim Janik, Heather Karban, Keith Karban, Laura Karban, Emily Mitchell, Ryan Mitchell, Mark Phillips, Megan Phillips, Joshua Powers, Nathan Powers, Jeremiah Pyles, Jordan Stumpf, Rachel Swederska, Andrew Yount, and Erin Yount. My thanks to them and to their parents. One mother—Kim Amos—plays a supporting role in one of the pictures.

The children's workers and the staff of the Southwest Baptist Church, St. Louis, Missouri, graciously helped me in a number of ways. Beth Spies spent a long Saturday helping create some of the decorations in the photographs. Gail Pence reviewed my manuscript for clarity.

I appreciate the delightful drawings and patterns created for the book by Ronald Kilkenney.

A special "thank you" to the staff of McFarland & Company, Inc., for the opportunity to fulfill my dream of some day writing a book!

British Library Cataloguing-in-Publication data are available

Library of Congress Cataloguing-in-Publication Data

Amos, Janell Shride, 1938–
    Entertaining children : theme parties, activities, games and fun
ideas for groups / by Janell Shride Amos.
        p.   cm.
    Includes index.
    ISBN 0-89950-738-7 (sewn softcover : 55# alk. paper) ∞
    1. Children's parties—Handbooks, manuals, etc.   2. Games—
Handbooks, manuals, etc.   3. Entertaining—Handbooks, manuals, etc.
I. Title.
GV1205.A46   1992
793.2′1—dc20   92-50300
                                                                              CIP

Manufactured in the United States of America

McFarland & Company, Inc., Publishers
    Box 611, Jefferson, North Carolina 28640

Contents

Introduction

Entertaining children can be very demanding. This book is designed to be used as a handbook by busy parents, grandparents, and others who spend time with children.

The parties, games and activities are all practical, as well as fun. The instructions are as brief as possible.

Keep in mind that many of the ideas adapt easily to fit a variety of circumstances. Be flexible!

Begin collecting the materials used in the activities I suggest, keep this book handy, and you will begin enjoying your status as a survivor of many rewarding hours spent entertaining the children in your life.

1. Complete Party Plans

A theme can add to the excitement and pleasure of any children's party. The theme can be expressed through the invitations, decorations, games and activities, prizes and favors, and the refreshments. Ideas for executing three themes are provided in this chapter. More games and activities are suggested than you can or should use so that you can select those most appropriate for the age and number of your guests.

When planning and leading games for children, be sure that:

- a quiet game/activity follows every one or two active games
- everyone understands how to play before you begin; you may need a practice round or a demonstration
- all play by the rules
- everyone has a turn
- the game moves quickly
- the activity is changed if it appears to be getting out of hand or many of the children lose interest
- all game "props" are ready ahead of time
- more games are planned than you expect to use—in case you need them
- all the children have moments of success and approval during the activities.

Preparing for a Party

Writing down plans and making lists of tasks to be done can result in having a more organized party and contribute to your enjoyment of the event.

Plan with your child and list the children you plan to invite. Beginning when the children are about eight years old, consider all boy or all girl parties.

Prepare and issue invitations, requesting an R.S.V.P., one or two weeks before the party date. Include a definite ending and beginning time (1½ to 2½ hours is about right for most children's parties). Enclose a map to your house, if you feel many of the parents will need it. If you are serving lunch or dinner, include that information in your invitation.

Select the games and activities you want to have at the party. Make a list of the games in the order you plan to play them.

List the items you need to collect or buy for the games. Decide what party area will be used for each activity. Be sure and consider the size of your play area, the ages of your guests, and the size of the party when planning your games and activities. Plan and purchase items for favors and name tags.

Decide how you will decorate and list the items you need to collect or purchase. Plan when you will do your decorating. There may be items you can prepare ahead of time to be put in place at the last minute. Who is available to help with the decorating? Enlist adult or teenage helpers and discuss with them what you need them to do before, during, and after the party. Plan how the children in your home can help with the preparations.

Decide what you will serve for refreshments and make a shopping list. Select foods to prepare ahead of time and those which must be prepared at the last minute. What dishes and serving items will you need? You may want to borrow some of the things you have on your purchase lists.

Go shopping with all the lists you have made of things to purchase. Consider going to a store that specializes in offering the type of things you are buying at reasonable prices (perhaps one that sells in bulk).

Organize the things you have collected and purchased for the party by dividing them into decorations, prizes and favors, game props and food items. Put them in a place that is away from curious young fingers. Prepare your game props and package the party favors as soon as possible. If you have children, include them and make the work a time of fun. You'll need the final hours before the party to decorate and finish making refreshments.

KEEPING KOOL PARTY

This theme is designed for a party with the children in swimsuits and thongs and may be held near a swimming pool or in a backyard with a handy water hose for cleaning up. Invitations specify that every-one brings spare clothes.

Invitations

Prepare the invitation information below. It can be photocopied or hand written on plain or blue paper. Fill in the information. Note the ready-to-copy invitation layout. If you do not have access to a copy machine, have copies made at a copy shop. Keep in mind that the copies can be enlarged, if you wish.

Come to a

KEEPING KOOL PARTY

Wear a bathing suit; bring spare clothes
and a towel; be prepared to get wet.

Date _____

Time _____

Host _____

Address_____

R.S.V.P. by calling _____

Another choice for invitations is to fold a sheet of heavy paper in half, position the pattern for the inner tube on your paper with the dotted line on the fold, and cut two identical shapes joined at the fold. Draw the ropes on the front as shown and write (or glue a copy of) the invitation information inside.

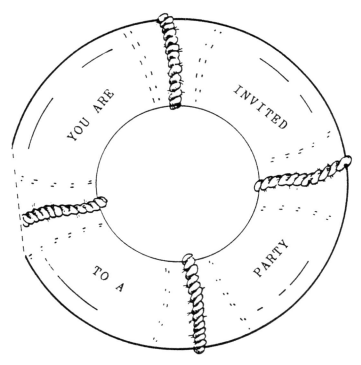

If you can hand deliver the invitations or you are willing to invest in big padded envelopes and postage, attach the invitations to plastic sun visors, sunglasses, or tubes of suntan lotion.

Decorations

Have signs decorated with balloons or beach balls directing guests to the outside party area and the dressing area. Small tents for changing clothes and storing dry clothes would be fun and they can have beach or other colorful towels draped over them.

Borrow extra beach towels from family and friends; use them to decorate and later for drying people and items that will surely be wet during and at the end of the party.

Blow up beach balls and other swimming inflatables and place them around the party area to add color and atmosphere. These may go home at the end of the party as favors.

Games and Activities

More games and activities are suggested than you can, or should, use for one party. Choose those best suited for the number and the ages of the children who will be present. Also take into consideration the size and arrangement of your outside party area.

Shooting Range: Decorate three small foam cups with bright suns and or flowers and line them up on a fence, picnic table or bench, or some other flat area which can tolerate being wet. Let the children take turns using a water pistol to try to shoot the cups down. Three tries make a turn. If you have several children, set up more than one shooting range; provide an adult or teenager to supervise each of your areas.

Shooting ranges can also be set up to shoot out lit candles, make pinwheels turn, or to shoot ping pong balls off the top of soda bottles (see photo on page 6). Spray bottles filled with water—perhaps colored with food coloring—can substitute for water pistols.

Shades Pin On: Attach a poster of someone in a bathing suit to a wall. Provide each child with a colorful pair of construction paper sunshades. At their turn, blindfold each player and see who can "pin on" the sunshades closest to the eyes of the sunbather. A sunbather for this game may be found on a beach towel, a travel poster, or a purchased poster. If you want to make you own sunbather, outline a child on a piece of long wrapping paper and draw on the features and bathing suit. Be prepared to attach the sunshades with straight pins or tape.

Water Carry: Place the children in a row at a beginning line and help each balance a foam cup of water on the back of their right hand. Players are to walk carefully to a goal line, use their teeth only to transfer the cup of water from the back of their right hand to the back of their left hand, and return to the beginning line. Winners are those who keep the water in their cup.

Shooting Range (with pinwheels).

Jump the Water Stream: Children take turns jumping over a stream of water from a water hose. If the water touches them, they drop out of the game. The stream of water is higher for each successive round of jumps. The winner is the last player to avoid getting wet from the water stream. This game can be played in reverse by having the players limbo under the water stream which gets progressively lower.

Slippery Slide: Spread a large plastic drop cloth or old shower curtains out on the yard. Weight the edges with bricks or large stones or anchor the corners with tent pegs covered with buckets for protection. Use a water hose or sprinkler to wet the plastic cloth/curtains. This provides a place for children to slip, slide, and play on a hot day. Protect the lawn by moving the slide frequently.

Pennies Search: Wrap at least five pennies per child in aluminum foil and hide them in a sandbox, a bale of hay, a bucket of bird seed, or a container of mud. At the signal, the children have a treasure hunt searching for the pennies.

Balloon Bop: Give each child an inflated and tied balloon and see who can keep it in the air the longest. When hitting it with their hands gets old, have them "bop" their balloons with their heads, elbows, knees, and or shoulders. Keep the children spread out over the playing area to reduce collisions.

Marbles and Toes: Have a race with the contestants carrying a marble between their toes. Be sure the racing area is friendly to bare feet.

Whipped Cream Fun: If you want to provide children with an extravagant (and probably a once-in-a-lifetime) experience, let them play with whipped cream. If possible, use spray cans of whipped cream, but whipped topping applied with fingers or plastic knives will work. Vary the activity to fit your group. Any age can use a dull plastic knife to "shave" cream from a balloon or slick paper plate. Older girls can shave their legs; boys can shave their chest and tummy. Supply a mirror and see who can create the best beard on themselves or a partner. The kids will find it hard to believe they can play with such a normally forbidden, messy substance. Plan how everyone will clean up. I suggest a water hose. Have towels handy.

Musical Sponge: While standing or sitting in a circle, players pass around a wet sponge. The child holding the sponge each time a whistle blows drops out of the game, the last one left wins.

Tug of War: Divide the players into two teams and have a standing or seated tug of war with a lawn sprinkler in the middle ready to sprinkle the losers (see photo on page 8). Choose a strong, but smooth, rope which will not damage hands.

Tug of War.

Water Balloon Toss: Designate partners and have them stand facing each other—two feet apart. Give each set of partners a water-filled
balloon to toss to each other (see photo on page 9). If the partners toss
their balloon without breaking it at two feet apart, they back up to be
three feet apart and toss the balloon. After each toss, they move a foot
further apart. The winning partners are those who successfully toss
their balloon the furthest distance without bursting it. Unless you have
a very large group, have the tosses made one at a time so everyone can
watch the fun.

The same activity using a raw egg would also be good for this outside "it's o.k. to get messy" party.

Feed the Monkey: One player sits in a chair with his hands behind
his back. His partner is blindfolded and given the task of peeling and
feeding him a banana. Several sets of partners can compete to see who
can most quickly complete their task of eating all of the banana. An ice
cream cone, a snow cone, or a jar of baby food fruit could be used instead of the banana.

Bottles of Water Relay: Team members pass identical bottles full
of water from person to person. The bottle should have no lid or

Top: Water Balloon Toss; *bottom:* Bottles of Water Relay.

stopper and be turned upside down at all times (see photo on page 9). The winner is the team with the most water still in the bottle when it reaches the last person. Try to find clear plastic bottles for this event. Two-liter soda bottles work well.

Ice Cube Relay: Each member of the team must carry an ice cube on a plastic knife, spatula, or ruler from a beginning line to a goal line and back. If the cube is dropped, the player must start again. This game could also be a race with all the children competing with each other.

Fill the Bottle Relay: One member of each team sits beside a full bucket of water holding a plastic soda bottle on his head. Each team has identical measuring cups. The team members take turns pouring one measuring cup of water from the bucket into the bottle on their player's head. The first team to fill their bottle wins. Plastic trash cans are good substitutes if you do not have buckets.

Sponge Squeeze Relay: Place a bucket full of water for each team at a goal line. At the beginning line place an empty bucket for each team. Provide teams with identical large sponges. The players take turns running to the goal line, soaking their sponge, running back to the beginning line, and squeezing their sponge into the team's bucket. The winners are the team with the most water in their beginning line bucket when time is called. Use a measuring cup to measure the water. A dishpan, large bowls, or other water-proof containers can be substituted for the buckets.

Prizes and Favors

Appropriate favors and prizes include water guns, pinwheels, pails and shovels, sunglasses, visors, tubes of sunblock, inflatable beach balls, bottles of bubbles with blowers, shaped sponges, Japanese fans for girls, and balls (see photo on page 11).

Refreshments

Cold refreshments are needed. Suggestions are snow cones, Popsicles, homemade or store bought ice cream, and watermelon slices. Have lots of cold drinks such as fruit punch and lemonade served in large paper cups over ice. Ice water should also be available.

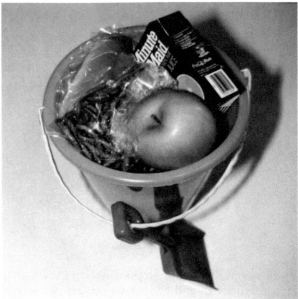

Top: Favors—pails and shovels; *bottom:* Refreshments—meal in a pail.

Barbequed hamburgers and hot dogs fit the setting of this party. For a prepare-ahead meal, put sandwiches or fried chicken and individual packages of chips, carrot sticks, and pieces of fruit in a pail with several napkins for clean up (see photo on page 11). Spread colorful shower curtains or plastic tablecloths to eat on. Don't forget the large garbage bag for trash clean up.

Alternate Plan

Make an alternate plan in case the party cannot take place outside due to rain or excessive heat.

I suggest having the party inside and using some of the following activities:

> Shades Pin On
> Balloon Bop (in a small area have 3 players at a time and have play-offs)
> Marbles and Toes
> Musical Sponge (use a dry sponge)
> Ice Cube Relay (with mop handy)—or substitute wrapped candy
> Pennies Search (with the pennies hidden in a room)
> Feed the Monkey (line the floor with old newspapers)

Use the planned decorations and eat picnic style on the floor.

M&Ms AND NUTS PARTY

This party will provide the perfect time for children to call each other a silly name—"M&M" or "Nut." The theme is not tied to any season or occasion so it is suitable for any time of the year.

Invitations

Prepare a copy of the invitation information shown on page 13 for each person you are inviting. If the invitations are delivered in person, you might tape the information to a small pack of M&Ms or peanuts. Or...

You are invited to an
M&Ms AND NUTS PARTY!

Date: _____

Time: _____

Place: _____

Host: _____

Construction paper sheets can be folded in half and a round shape or a peanut shape cut so that there are identical shapes still joined at the left side. Decorate the top shape as an M&M or a peanut with a face, or glue or tape a real M&M and a nut to it; tape or glue the sheet giving the invitation facts inside so it can be read when the top shape is lifted. If you plan to mail your invitations, consider how the construction paper shape will fit in your envelopes before you determine the size of your cutout shape. The pattern (see page 15) is provided as a guide for the peanut-shaped invitations. It is ready to copy. Use a plate or other round object if you do round shapes.

Add the following sentences to your invitation—or enclose them on a separate piece of paper—if you wish to do the Gallery of Little Nuts activity (see page 17):

Bring a baby picture of yourself in an envelope or sack.
Don't let anyone see your picture since it will be part of a game.

Decorations

Buy bright colored paper plates in M&M colors and decorate them with a white "M." Create nut people from brown construction paper and pipe cleaners. Make mobiles from the plates and nut figures by hanging them at different lengths with the strings going through a stabilizing top plate. Suspend the mobiles from light fixtures and or doorways (see photo on page 16).

Cut brown and tan construction paper or wrapping paper into the shapes of peanuts in the shell, walnuts and pecans. Add faces, arms, legs, hats, etc., to give them personality and tape them to the walls of the party area.

Use the M&M cakes (see photo on page 24) or make Mr. and Mrs. Coconuts for a table centerpiece. A brown twin sheet would make an effective tablecloth. Serve the food on the same color of paper plates being used for the mobiles.

Games and Activities

For all activities using teams, divide your group into the M&Ms and the Nuts. If you wish to have more than two groups, have Red M&Ms, Yellow M&Ms, Peanuts, Pecans, etc. You might lay M&Ms

Shaped invitation pattern to copy.

and nuts on numbered slips of paper and let the guests draw a number from a bowl to see if they are a Nut or an M&M; of course, each gets to eat the candy or nut which is on his/her numbered slip.

Nut Hunt: Hide assorted unshelled nuts in a designated area. Assign values to each kind of nut and tell the players the values. For

M&Ms and Nuts mobile.

example: peanuts = 1 point; pecans = 2 points; walnuts = 3 points. Give each team a bowl or basket. At a signal, all players from both teams find as many hidden nuts as they can and put them in their team's bowl. The points earned for each kind of nut collected are totaled and a winning team declared. If the children are old enough, have a follow-up contest to see which team can produce the most shelled nuts in the time allowed. You'll need to supply tools to crack the nuts or have an adult do the cracking for each team. Collecting the shelled nuts in measuring cups will make it easy to determine the winner.

Nut on Toe Relay: Team members must all walk to a goal line and back with a nut in a shell balanced on the toe of one shoe. If the nut is dropped, the player returns to the beginning spot and begins again. The team which first has all its members complete the task wins.

M&Ms on a Knife Relay: Teams race to have each team member carry six M&Ms on a plastic knife to a goal line and back without dropping any (see photo on page 18). Of course, no hands may touch the M&Ms.

Peanut Carry Relay: Each player places three unshelled peanuts on the back of a hand and walks to a goal line and back. If any peanut drops, the player must start again from the beginning line.

Spoon Pass Relay: Give each player a plastic spoon to be held in his/her mouth. An M&M or peanut is passed from spoon to spoon down the line of players on each team. No hands can be used (see photo on page 18). Dropping the M&M or peanut requires the team to begin again with the first player.

Gallery of Little Nuts: If your invitations asked the children to bring a baby picture, have an adult collect them as the children arrive and—in another room—use masking tape to mount the pictures on a bright colored poster board (see photo on page 19). Place a number by each picture. When you are ready to do this activity, bring out the picture poster board.

For younger children, caution them to not tell which picture is theirs during the guessing, and then have them take turns telling who they think the baby is in one of the pictures. After the guessing is completed, let each child point out his/her baby picture

For older children, have them write on a piece of paper who they think each baby picture belongs to—using the numbers by the pictures to identify their guesses. Name tags are needed during this activity, unless you are sure that every child playing knows and can spell the names of all the children present. After the guesses are written on the papers, collect them and check them as the children identify their baby picture. The praise and or prize goes to the child with the most correct answers.

Elephant Feed: Draw an elephant's head and trunk on a poster board, cut out a hole for a mouth, and have the children see who can

Top: M&Ms on a Knife Relay; *bottom:* Spoon Pass Relay.

Gallery of Little Nuts.

throw the most peanuts through the elephant's mouth (see a scaled-down model on page 20). Use masking tape to mark the place to stand while throwing. Ten peanuts in the shell to throw is about right for a turn.

What Am I?: Pin the name of a nut or the color of an M&M on the back of each child. Each player tries to find out what is on his/her back by asking other players questions that can only be answered with "yes" or "no." Answers given must be truthful. Cover any mirrors in the game area during this activity.

Find That Nut: While one player is out of the room, the others hide a walnut. The player is called back into the room and tries to find the nut while the others help by calling out "Cold" if the hunter moves away from the nut and "Warm" or "Hot" if he moves closer to the nut.

The Candy Monster and the M&M Candy: A child is chosen to be the Candy Monster and is blindfolded. Another player becomes the M&M Candy. All the other players form a circle with the Candy Monster and the M&M Candy in the middle. The Monster tries to catch the Candy. At any time the Monster can stand still and call "Yum Yum." The Candy must answer "M&M." If the Candy is too successful in not being caught, the circle should be made gradually smaller. New players are selected for several rounds of play.

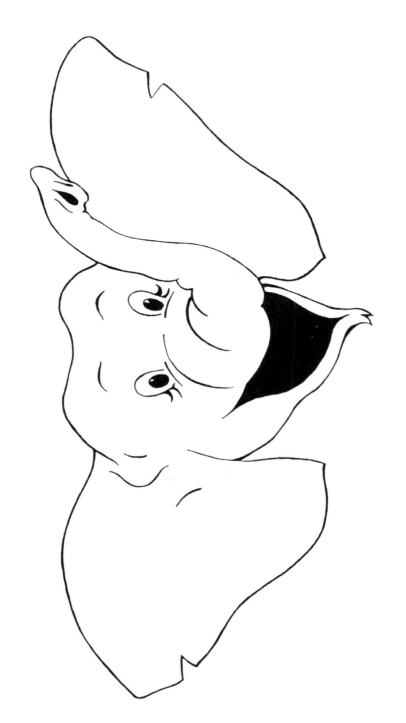

Elephant Feed pattern.

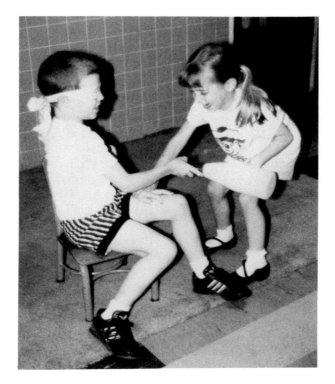

Nutty Nut.

Nutty Nut: Blindfold a player and seat him/her on a stool or stack of cushions in the center of the playing area with a fly swatter, foam bat, or a rolled up newspaper. Two or three at a time the other players sneak up on the person in the center while saying "Nutty-Nut" every few seconds. The goal is for the blindfolded player to swat one of the sneakers. Anyone swatted becomes "It" and the game continues.

Squirrels, Gophers and Chipmunks. Seat all players except "It" in a circle. Name each player squirrel, gopher, or chipmunk. Blindfold the player who is "It," place him/her in the center, and give him/her a foam bat or a rolled up newspaper. Tell everyone that "It" is trying to knock out all the squirrels, gophers and chipmunks in the yard in order to protect his/her supply of nuts. "It" calls out "squirrels," "gophers" or "chipmunks." All the players named the animal called must change seats when their name is called. While they are finding a different seat,

"It" is trying to swat them with the foam bat or newspaper. When some-one is hit, that person becomes "It" and play continues. The game leader has the job of letting "It" know when everyone has found a seat and that it is time to call out "squirrels," "gophers," or "chipmunks" again.

Don't Crush the M&Ms: Scatter M&Ms on the floor or ground between a beginning line and a goal line. Divide the players into part-ners. One player is to be blindfolded while the other verbally guides him/her through the M&Ms. If an M&M is touched by a foot, that set of partners drops out of the game. After the first round, reverse roles and blindfold the players who did the guiding for a second round of the game. Try this game with the children barefooted and walk-ing on a painting drop cloth or an old shower curtain. If you don't want to use real M&Ms for the game, use some made of construction paper.

Hiding Places: Gather the children around you and have them help you think of all the places they could hide M&Ms and Nuts as you write them on a poster (see photo on page 23). Starting with A, and then B, and then C, etc., see if the group can think of at least one hiding place for each letter of the alphabet. At the end of the game you might want to vote on which hiding place would be the hardest to find, which is the funniest place to hide something, and which is the most unusual hiding place. Sample answers are—Attic, Book, Crayon box, Dog house, etc.

Prizes and Favors

Use individual size sacks of M&Ms, peanuts, cashew nuts, and mixed nuts for prizes and favors. Mix M&Ms, nuts, pretzel pieces, and cereals toasted in spices and butter. Place the mixture in small plastic bags and tie the tops in bright colored ribbons.

Puzzles, coloring or activity books, crayons, magic slates, paper dolls, model airplanes, or craft kits make great take-home and "do later" prizes and favors.

Make tiny turtles from walnut shells with construction paper head and feet. Place one at each place at the table and then send them home with each child as a favor.

Hiding Places.

Refreshments

Small triangle peanut butter sandwiches surrounded by fruit slices and chunks make an appropriate beginning course for this party. Feature round chocolate cakes with bright colored icing. Decorate the cakes with big icing Ms or real M&M candies (see photo on page 24). Serve small individual cups of mixed nuts for the children who like nuts. Milk with food coloring and a touch of vanilla would complement these foods.

M&M cake.

SNOWMAN LAND PARTY

A Snowman Land Party is a good theme for anytime in the winter. The activities are all suitable for inside. Set the tone of the party by playing Frosty the Snowman as guests arrive and leave.

Invitations

Use the pattern provided to create invitations in the shape of snowmen which open up to show the party information. Color the snowman's hat and facial features black and the scarf and broom bright colors — such as red, blue, or green. Emphasize the color(s) you plan to

Snowman Land party invitation pattern.

use as the decorating scheme. The pattern above can be used to photo-copy a shape pattern for the invitations.

Copy (or glue copies of) the information on page 26 inside the snowman shape.

You are invited
to a party in

SNOWMAN LAND

Located at_____

Date _____   Time_____

Call _____

At _____

to let us know you are coming.

Invitation information for Snowman Land party.

Decorations

Create ahead of time, or with the help of the children, a big snowman using three sheets of poster board or a large piece of foam board cut into snowman shape. Have on hand or make hats and scarves for the snowman. Use felt or construction paper for facial features and buttons. Be sure everyone knows the name of your snowman. Make smaller snowmen and snow women on poster board and attach them to the walls of the party area. These decorations will serve as patterns for the children if you do the "Snowman Friend Skits."

To contrast with the white of the snowmen in the decorations and refreshments, use a bright color such as red, blue or green as part of your decorating scheme. Have some items such as construction paper place mats, napkins, snowman scarves, balloons, punch, etc., in the color you have chosen. Use napkin rings decorated with small construction paper snowmen. Three different sizes of small Styrofoam balls can be made into cute snowmen/snow women favors for each child by adding painted features and hats or scarves. (see page 27).

For the table centerpiece, make a popcorn snowman held together with frosting and toothpicks. Make the hat, face, scarf, and buttons of candy, colored miniature marshmallows, chocolate chips, red and green cherries, etc. You might want to draw names to see which child takes this home.

Snowmen/snow women favors.

Games and Activities

Snowman Walk: Cut two snowman shapes from poster board or heavy paper for each player or team. The player stands on one snowman while throwing the second one in front of him/her (see photo on page 28). This process is repeated until a goal line is reached. If either foot touches the ground rather than staying on a snowman, the player must return to the beginning point and try again. The snowman shapes should be bigger than any player's shoe, but not big enough to stand on with both feet. Hands may be used on the floor or ground for balance.

Marshmallow Feed: Marshmallows are placed in two big bowls or aluminum pie plates on a chair or table. Each player on each team runs to the team's bowl of marshmallows, scoops up one with a spoon held in the mouth and carefully carries it back and feeds it to the next person in line, who then goes for a marshmallow for the next child, etc. The winning team is the one which first completes feeding all of their marshmallows to members of their team.

Snowman Walk.

Snowman Friend Skits: Divide the children into groups with three or four in each group and tell them to plan and practice a skit about a magic snowman who becomes a friend of a group of children.

They are to draw the snowman who is part of the skit on a large poster board or sheet of paper. Provide the supplies the children will need. (If you don't want to take time for the groups to make a snowman, have one decorating the walls for each group and give each group one of your snowmen.)

The snowman must have a name and an explanation of what happens in order for him to be magical and able to talk to the children. It might be certain circumstances — like it being 6:00 A.M. on a Saturday — or a song or a rhyme or passwords that must be said before the Snowman can talk.

After the group has created their snowman, named him, and

Snowman Friend Skits.

decided what magic lets him talk, they are ready to plan the events in their skit.

The skit should have a part for each member of the group; one of them should hold their snowman and speak for him. The skit should be about something good the snowman does for the children. Try to let the groups shape their own skit but, if they seem "stuck," give each group a different suggestion, such as:

- the snowman helps find lost pets
- the snowman plays with a child being treated badly by his friends
- the snowman teaches the children a song and or dance
- the snowman tells them a favorite story with a surprise ending
- the snowman wants to live with them but learns he will melt if he goes inside
- the snowman answers questions about his permanent home at the North Pole

After the skits are planned, they are performed for everyone. If any adults are present, they become part of the audience. A video camera could provide a tape for the children to watch later.

Please note that this activity will take up most of the time of a normal length party. You will have time for only one or two other short activities if the children get "into" this project.

Snowman Drawing: Give each player a sheet of paper and a crayon or marker. Each player sits on the floor with his/her paper on the floor directly behind him/her. At a signal, each child draws a snowman behind his/her back without looking (see photo below). Award ribbons for the prettiest, funniest, most original, etc., snowman drawings. If the group size allows it, you may want to have as many categories as you have children so all win a ribbon. Tape the works of art on the walls for the rest of the party and then send them home with the children.

Snowman Drawing.

Snowball Carry: Using cotton balls or large marshmallows for snowballs, have a relay race requiring each team member to carry a "snowball" to a goal line and back on a ruler.

Snowball Throw: Obtain five plastic foam balls and number them 5, 10, 15, 20, and 25. Each child takes a turn pitching the five balls into a large bowl or other container (see photo below). Add up the numbers on the balls that land and stay in the bowl. The player with the highest score is the winner.

Snowball Throw.

Snowball Scoop.

Snowball Scoop: Seat a blindfolded child at a table containing a bowl of cotton balls and an empty bowl. The empty bowl should be about six inches from the bowl of cotton balls. Give the player a spoon and instruct him/her to dip the cotton balls from the bowl and dump them into the empty bowl. Give each child 2 minutes to work. The empty hand may be used to locate the bowls but may not touch the cotton balls or the spoon. After all players have had a turn, declare the one who dumped the most cotton balls into the empty bowl the winner.

Frosty the Snowman: Blindfold one player and sit him/her in a chair with his back to the other players. The game leader selects a player to sing two lines of the song "Frosty, the Snowman" while disguising his voice. The blindfolded player tries to identify the singer. If he does, the singer takes the place of the blindfolded person; if he doesn't, he tries to guess the identity of other singers until he is successful.

Don't Step on Snowy: Cut a snowman-shaped figure out of a large piece of paper or poster board. Write "Snowy" on the figure and tape it to the floor in the middle of the game area. Have everyone join hands in the circle around "Snowy." To begin the action, the game leader calls out "Don't step on Snowy!" and everyone tries to pull the other players onto Snowy. As soon as someone touches the Snowy figure, that child drops out of the game and the circle is reformed for another round. The one player who avoids stepping on Snowy is the winner.

Three Words in a Row: Give each player a pencil and a sheet of paper and have them divide their paper into three rows of three boxes (see photo below). Show them the following words written on a long strip of paper: OUR SNOWMAN HAS COAL EYES AND A CARROT NOSE. The sentence has nine words and the player's papers have nine squares. Tell the children to write each of the words in one of their squares; each child decides where to put each word. When everyone's paper is ready, tear your strip apart so that each word is on a separate piece of paper. Drop the words into a bowl, pull out one word at a time and read it to the players. They are to cross off the words on their paper as they are read. The first one who crosses off three in a row—across, down, or diagonally—is the winner.

Three Words in a Row.

Snowball Blow.

If the children want to play more than one round, use the following sentences or make up one of your own with nine words. "A Snowman Likes Cold Days and Dreads Warm Weather." "I Would Like to Name My Snowman Billy Jack."

Snowball Blow: Provide ping pong balls and have two or more children race their balls by blowing them across a long table or the floor (see photo above).

Prizes and Favors

Consider the following ideas for favors/prizes: the big snowman decoration, snowman centerpiece, Styrofoam snowman/snow woman (see photo on page 27), snowman cookies, gloves, scarves the color of the color scheme, stocking caps, white or clear marble sets, popcorn balls, tape recording or book of *Frosty the Snowman.*

Refreshments

Serve hot chocolate with marshmallow snowballs floating in the chocolate. Make snowman faces to eat by spreading soft cream cheese on party round bread or round slices of bread cut with a biscuit cutter and using raisins or black olives for features. Or serve biscuits sliced and stuffed with chicken chunks and salad dressing. Surround the sandwiches with fruit slices and or carrot sticks. Scoops of vanilla ice cream rolled in coconut and snowman or round sugar cookies would be a good dessert.

2. Party Theme Ideas

The descriptions for each suggested theme are brief and designed to "get you started" on planning a party with the theme. If you want more activities and ideas than those suggested, just browse through the other chapters of this book looking for other ideas to use as they are or to adapt to the theme.

A discussion about your party with the main child or a few of the children you plan to entertain should be very helpful in guiding your selection of a party theme and in deciding whether or not to invite both sexes. When they are about eight years old, children often begin to prefer all girl or all boy parties.

Genie in a Bottle

Make bottle-shaped invitations with the party theme and information printed on them. Have a large bottle, or a fancy bottle, on prominent display when guests arrive; tell the guests you have reason to believe a genie is trapped inside. For games have the children write down or name things they would ask a genie to give them. Try to make a list having at least one item for each letter of the alphabet. Have a genie drawing contest — ask "What do you think the genie in this bottle might look like?" Award prizes for the prettiest/most handsome, ugliest, and most unusual picture drawn. Place the bottle in front of the group of children and try various ways to get the genie to come out of the bottle. Make up genie names and say, for example, "Georgette come out!" and "Zoom come out!" Whether or not the children suggest it, try rubbing the bottle different ways. After a while, have the children turn around, close their eyes and say K-*zoom* slowly five times. While they are doing this, have someone "appear," playing the part of the genie. The person playing the genie needs a costume and some stories about how he/she got in the bottle and some tall tales about previous adventures. The genie can have the children sing songs, say rhymes or do sets of motions which might help bring back his/her powers. When it is time for refreshments, give the children noisemakers and send them on a marching route to scare away evil spirits, while the genie meditates and tries to regain his/her powers. When the children return, genie and bottle are gone, but a note from genie says, "My powers came back and forced me to leave. Thank you for helping me. I'll try to see you again some time." Packages of favors will have been left by the genie and the refreshments will be ready.

Camping Adventure

Have a slumber party in a camping setting. Use tents or recreational vehicles, or sleep in the open on sleeping bags on top of waterproof ground covers. Camp at a nearby park, campground, farm, or in a large backyard. A commercial campground may have a swimming pool and or a recreation room you can use with the children. Play some active games like three-legged races, or musical chairs using pieces of cardboard or newspaper on the ground instead of chairs, etc. After dark have a game of flashlight tag. Cook hotdogs and marshmallows over a campfire, if possible. Find short mystery stories in a library book to read or play a tape of old-time scary radio shows. Start a story and, at a signal, have a designated child continue the story. You bring it to a conclusion after several have contributed. Be sure at least a couple of the adults involved have experience camping. Expect to forget something you'll need; that is part of camping fun.

Ghost Gathering

Invite guests to arrive wrapped in an old white sheet or tablecloth. Pin names of animals or cartoon characters on everyone's back. Have each player go up to every other child—once only—and ask "Who-o-o am I?" The player asked must supply a clue. As each person discovers his/her identity, a prize is given. Play a scrambled word game with the words being things found in a haunted house. Create an obstacle course and have a ghost friend verbally guide each blindfolded player around the obstacles. Show everyone a table of assorted small items; under cover of a white cloth remove an item and see if players can tell what you removed. Decorate with ghosts made from old sheets or tablecloths or crepe paper tied over a ball and suspended from wall hangars or door frames. Make ghost favors and decorations by covering suckers with Kleenex and painting on faces. You might take a Casper—the Friendly Ghost, or a Ghost Busters approach to this theme.

Parade Time

Provide supplies and have the children decorate bicycles, tricycles, wagons and other toys on wheels which can be ridden or pulled. Form a rhythm marching band with real and homemade instruments. Have the children practice playing and marching to suitable music played by a portable tape player. When all is ready, parade around the neighborhood. Be sure and take lots of pictures! End with refreshments and clean up time.

Cooking Party

Many foods can be the focus of a cooking party. Provide the ingredients in an organized state and aprons or big shirts to protect clothes. If the guests will eat their creation, I suggest individual pizzas. Allow the children to make dough, add ingredients to taste, and create a face with some of the toppings. Decorating cupcakes or making ice cream ball clowns with cone hats would provide a dessert. Make the dessert after the pizzas are cooked and eaten. Take pictures of the food creations with the cooks and award blue ribbon prizes for many categories. Eating and cleaning up are part of the entertainment. If the food cooked is not the party food, you might bake and decorate cookies or cakes for gifts for Mother's Day, Father's Day, or someone who is ill or a shut-in.

Balloon Blast

Insert the invitation in a balloon, blow it up, and write "POP ME" on the outside with a marker. If you need to invite by mail, make color-ful construction paper balloons to glue on a sheet of paper and write the invitations on the balloons or under them. Have the guests make clowns of balloons by drawing a face with a marker and slipping the tied end of the balloon through large cardboard feet with a slit in the mid-dle. Use the balloon clowns for decorations and as favors. Use balloons in your games. See who can keep their inflated balloon in the air the longest. Have everyone individually or as teams sit on balloons to pop them. Do relays such as carrying balloons between the knees and part-ners walking to a goal line carrying a balloon between their shoulders, between their foreheads, and or between their backs. Helium balloons would make good decorations and take-home favors.

Backwards Party

Send invitations which can be read by holding them in front of a mirror. Have guests enter by the back door; greet them with "goodbye." Everyone wears as many of their clothes as they can backwards. Right-handed children use their left hand and left-handed children use their right hand for games and eating. Refreshments may be served first. How about eating pineapple upside-down cake and sandwiches of bread between lunch meat while standing at the table. Pictures on the wall and decorations can be hung upside down. Give prizes for reciting the alphabet or nursery rhymes backwards; have a backward spelling bee; race backwards to a goal line; wrap favors with the paper inside out. Just do the opposite of the normal for many of the activities.

Indian Pow Wow

Build a totem pole of big tin cans with lids. Let the beginning ac-tivity be decorating the cans by covering them and decorating them with Indian faces and designs. Make tom-toms by cutting both ends from a coffee can, or other can, and covering the ends with strong round balloons secured by heavy rubber bands or elastic; use construc-tion paper to give the tom-toms an Indian look. Supplies like large pieces of construction paper, wallpaper, shelf lining, markers, scissors, glue, tape, egg boxes, paper cups, macaroni, big buttons, felt scraps, and the like, should be on hand for use. Give everyone a headband with a feather and play follow the leader in a war or rain dance around the totem pole to the beat of the tom-toms. Relays using rocks or leaves would fit the theme. Have some thumb and arm wrestling contests. Brown sack pouches filled with trail mix and corn candy would be a good favor or snack. Serve buffalo burgers as the main course if you have a meal.

For Girls Only

Have teenagers or adults available to give manicures, apply makeup, and paint a flower on a cheek, leg or arm. Provide a big assortment of dress-up clothes, such as high heels, skirts that will be long on the girls, hats, scarves, gloves, and costume jewelry. Allow each girl to create her own unique outfit and then have a fashion show with a video camera and play it back for the girls. For refreshments, try a tea party after the fashion show but before they return to their normal clothes.

Clue Caper or Dick Tracy Party

Invite the guests to arrive in disguise. They might wear a wig, false mustache, or dark glasses. Give a prize for the person who was most successful in changing his/her appearance. Hide many pennies in a game area and tell the players to find and collect as many as they can during the time allowed. To make it more interesting, identify the pennies made in one particular year as taboo; anyone who turns in a penny for that year cannot win a prize. If you want to give magnifying glasses as favors, have them used during the penny's game. Have the players take turns moving one object in a room while everyone else is gone. Whoever guesses what was moved first, makes the change for the next round. Any game involving finding things or using clues would be good for this party theme. Decorate with the names of television detectives and police officers. Display copies of Nancy Drew, Hardy Boys, and other mystery stories. Use name tags shaped like police badges. Provide a series of clues which lead to the refreshment site.

Treasure Hunt

Design the invitation to resemble a treasure map with the X indicating your address. Plan two or three games involving finding hidden objects which the children can keep or swap for a prize. Then supply old magazines, divide the children into groups of three or four, and have them find pictures in the magazines of things you have listed on a piece of paper. For example, they can look for a red car, running shoes, or a coat. Give prizes to the group which locates the most pictures of items in the time given. The main event should be a treasure hunt with clues. These are fairly easy to do if you select the places to hide the clues and

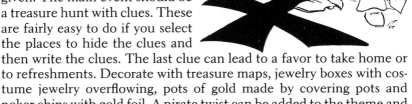

then write the clues. The last clue can lead to a favor to take home or to refreshments. Decorate with treasure maps, jewelry boxes with costume jewelry overflowing, pots of gold made by covering pots and poker chips with gold foil. A pirate twist can be added to the theme and involve pirate hats, headbands, and eye patches.

Trip to Mexico

Creating a Mexican atmosphere will be easier if you can obtain decorations from someone who has visited the Southwest or Mexico, a Spanish teacher, or a store stocking one or more basic items such as bright pottery or cacti. Travel agents might be a source of literature or posters, especially if you can catch them with items going out of date. You can make the children serapes (brightly colored blankets or shawls) and give them cactus plants used as decorations for favors. Play musical chairs using taped Spanish-style music or the beat of a rhythm instrument. Pin the tail on a donkey with a Mexican hat. Have "It" try to identify an object chosen by the group by asking questions which must be answered "si" for yes and "no" for no. Make a target in the shape of a map of Mexico and let the children earn a prize if they can throw a penny within two inches of the capitol city. Serve tacos with a backup of sloppy joe sandwiches for those who do not like tacos, or have a mild chili with crackers.

Mud Hole Day

If you have access to an empty garden spot, turn it into a mud hole for a party. All the children should wear old clothes and bring a change of clothes. Plan for the use of a water hose clean-up area and a place for changing clothes after the party. It is important that all parents understand what you have in mind for this party. Plow or otherwise loosen the dirt where you plan to have your mud hole and then flood it with water. Use a long piece of clothesline for a tug of war over the mud hole. Have a contest for making mud sculptures on a paper plate base. Hide plastic animals or figures in the mud and give a prize to the child or team who finds the most or particular ones. After the mud play serve "Delicious Dirt" for dessert. (See recipe below.) This could be a wonderful event for preschool age children if there is plenty of adult or teenage supervision. It does require warm and fairly dry weather, so a backup plan would be needed.

Delicious Dirt

Cream 11 ounces of cream cheese and ½ cup of soft margarine; add 1 cup of powdered sugar, 12 ounces of whipped topping, and 2 packages of instant vanilla pudding mixed with 3 cups of milk. Alternate layers of this mixture with a pound of crushed Oreo cookies. Put the dessert in a bucket and serve it with a small shovel. Add gummy worms for a great effect.

Indoor Picnic

This theme will be most welcome in the winter. Decorate with a big golden sun and for the first activity have the children make large construction paper flowers to add to the atmosphere. If you have room, play picnic-type games like tag and hide-and-seek and three-legged races. Blindfold a player who has a stuffed teddy bear in his/her lap and have him or her try to swat with a foam bat or rolled newspaper the different momma and papa bears trying, one at a time, to steal the teddy bear. Put a tablecloth on the floor with a collection of picnic containers, food and paper products on it. Have one blindfolded child at a time feel the items and try to guess what they are. Give sunglasses, straw hats, or balls for favors. Serve the food picnic-style on the floor — perhaps in individual baskets or boxes.

Gypsy Camp

Invite everyone to come dressed as a gypsy. Be sure the adults and teenagers who are helping with the party are in costume. As they arrive, provide the children with play money or poker chips to give the gypsies for their fortunes and to play the various games which are set up. A fortune teller should have a crystal ball (upside down fishbowl with silver paper ball) or be able to read cards or palms or tea leaves. The fortune teller should have in mind *happy* fortune cookie or horoscope type fortunes to share with the children when she tells their fortunes.

Have a series of contests/games set up in different locations and let the children move from one to the other. Give prizes for the various activities as you would at a school carnival. Chapter 3 of this book will give you many ideas to select from. Costume jewelry and bright colored sashes or T shirts would be good favors and add to the gypsy atmosphere. Rig tent-looking booths for the fortune teller and carnival games using colored sheets, bedspreads, and the like. A cooking pot and mock campfire would be good focus decorations.

Toy Shop

Younger children do well with a simple party plan. Have a play area filled with toys and call it your Toy Shop. Allow the children some free time playing with the toys as everyone arrives. If you do not have toys of your own, borrow some or consider having your party at a church nursery or a nursery school after hours. For games, scatter some of the larger toys in the middle of the floor and then lead a game of follow-the-leader winding around the toys. Walk in different ways (like a duck, while patting your head, while clapping your hands, while touching your knees, for example). Toss large, soft balls into a laundry basket to win a prize. Let the children take turns hiding a specific toy in the toy shop for the other children to find. The one who finds the toy hides it for the next round. Blindfold all of the children and let them try to catch "It" who is not blindfolded but must stay in the toy shop. Keep the party short and try to have some helpers ready to keep the games going smoothly.

Pioneer Party

Make simple cloth or construction paper sun bonnets for the girls and give the boys bandannas to wear around their necks. Give everyone a pencil and paper and then blindfold them. Ask everyone to draw a horse; when everyone finishes, tell them to add a saddle; have everyone draw a man sitting in the saddle; and last, ask for a hat on the head of the man. After the masterpieces are displayed, give a prize for the best drawing and a prize for the funniest drawing. Use plastic cowboy and Indian sets for decorations, favors and games. For a relay, have players race to a goal line with a small cowboy balanced on the toe of one shoe and a small Indian balanced on the other. Draw a target shaped like a wagon wheel with spokes and see who can earn the most points tossing plastic cowboys and Indians at the target. Pass a "crying" baby in a blanket around a circle while a harmonica or other music is played. The player with the baby when the music stops drops out each round. Decorate the table with a covered wagon full of favors. Make the covered wagon by attaching a poster board top to a toy wagon or a wagon made of a box with cardboard wheels and tongue. Serve chili or baked beans with slices of hot dogs in aluminum pie pans for a main course.

3. Skill Challenges

The activities in this chapter require a skill which can be improved with practice. The practice is often as much fun as the contest. One child can work to improve his/her best score. Several children can play the game at the same time if you have several sets of the materials needed. Teams can do the contests one at a time to earn scores and perhaps a prize for their team. Skill challenge activities can be operated at the same time with the children moving from one to the other.

Many of the ideas in this chapter can also be adapted for use in a booth at a school or club carnival. Always try out the activity you set up to be sure it works as you intend; if possible, have a child the age you plan to use the activity with help you test your challenge. Adjust distances, heights, number of tries, and such to match your circumstances and the age and skill of the participants.

See "Balloon Stomp," page 56.

45

Throw-Into Challenges: A number of items can be used for skill challenges which require throwing smaller items into some type of container (see photo below). This kind of activity is also usually interesting to teenagers and adults who play with the children. Give a reward for each successful throw or award points which earn awards or privileges for longer games or a series of games. It is best if everyone wins something. Be sure you try your game ahead of time. State the number of throws, where each person must stand, and how prizes will be awarded in a clear manner. Act as though the rules are very precise, even though you made them up.

Items to Throw	*Things to Throw Into*
new pennies	muffin tins
metal washers	aluminum foil pans
beans	egg containers
buttons	coffee cans
poker/game chips	bowls of varying sizes
nuts in the shell	big shoes
aluminum foil balls	flower pots

Items to Throw	*Things to Throw Into*
sock balls	sauce pans
balls of all kinds	jars
sponges	boxes
round plastic pan scratchers	laundry baskets
balloons	trash cans
paper plates	open umbrellas
bean bags	plates
playing cards	plastic milk crates
wrapped candy	

Throw-Through Challenges: Hang by a string or cord—from a clothesline, a clothes rack, a suspension rod in a doorway, or a broom or yardstick held by two people—a needlework hoop, a clothes hanger, a small swimming tube, or aluminum foil rolled and shaped into a hollow circle. Each player attempts to throw 3 to 5 straws, suckers, small plastic airplanes, paper airplanes, dowel rods, plastic pan scratchers, bean bags, or nerf balls through the opening from a mark established by a string, tape, or cardboard to stand on.

Another type of throw-through challenge is to prop up a cardboard face which has an opening for its mouth. The players attempt to throw objects such as bean bags, sponges, or balls through the opening. Jack-o-lantern pumpkins and clown faces are examples of props for this type of game. Draw the face on poster board or buy an appropriate large cardboard decoration and cut out a mouth opening. A frame the size of standard poster board is convenient for using to create this type of game to fit different themes. A face attached to a large cardboard box with a hole behind the mouth also works well.

Throw-Over Challenges: Provide rings made of rolled aluminum foil, cardboard, clothes hangers (tape over where the wire meets), rubber jar rings, curtain rings, needlework hoops, or bracelets. The rings may be thrown over bottle necks, prizes, pieces of candy, ring toss sticks, or small juice glasses with numbers inside. Prizes should be awarded based on success in "ringing" the target. If the ring is thrown over candy, let the candy serve as the prize.

Tennis Ball Bounce: Each player attempts to make three tennis balls bounce into a trash can, a laundry basket, a box, a dish pan, an open umbrella, a flower pot, or some other container. The ball must bounce; it cannot be thrown directly into the container. Any ball which bounces well may be used for this activity. In small areas try a jack ball bounced into a small container like a paper cup or bowl.

Clothespin Drop: This old game is easy to set up and usually popular with all ages. The goal is to hold a clothespin waist high and drop it into a bottle or jar. Each player should have four to six tries.

Baby Skill Contest: Provide each player with a baby bottle filled with water or juice. Use new nipples which release the liquid at the same speed. Have a contest to see which player can empty his/her bottle first by sucking on the nipple. If you have more children than bottles, have several groups and then have the winners of each group compete with each other.

Chopsticks Pick Up: Chopsticks are easy to obtain from oriental restaurants and stores and can be used for a number of skill challenges. For example, have a series of contests. Require that chopsticks be used with only one hand. Roll balloons to a goal line using only chopsticks. Move grapes from one bowl to another. Race to eat the contents of a small bowl of fried rice. Move jelly beans from one spot to another.

Coffee Can Croquet: Use a broom, mop handle, yardstick, or plastic bat to knock a small ball through a series of coffee cans which have both ends cut out and are lying on their sides (see photo on page 49).

Target Games: Award prizes and or points for success with the following games involving a variety of targets.

- Have pennies, game chips, or beans thrown at a calendar lying on a flat surface. Give points equal to the date on which the thrown object lands.
- Draw a target on newspaper, wrapping paper, or poster board and supply small items to be thrown at the target. Plastic pan scratchers, sponges, and bean bags all work well.
- Hang Christmas bells in a doorway from a hook or on a spring curtain rod. Challenge the players to ring the bell by hitting it with a ball made of soft material. Test your set-up thoroughly to be sure it can tolerate a barrage of enthusiastically thrown balls.
- Drop from chest height a cardboard shape about the size of a large hand on to a dime, button, or poker chip on the floor. The player should not bend over or use more than one hand. The shape may complement a party theme and or be decorated in a pretty design or color.

Coffee Can Croquet.

Paper Clip Chain: Give each player an equal number of paper clips. The winner is the first one to put all the paper clips together to form a chain.

Party Bowling: Line up ten 2-liter plastic soda bottles, half gallon milk jugs, or cans in bowling format and invite players to knock them down with a ball. Use masking tape to mark the spot for each bottle and the restraining line. Award prizes to the player who knocks down the most "pins." Have roll-offs for ties. Be sure and try your bowling set-up before the party to be sure it works well.

Hot Air Champ.

Gum Pick-Up: While wearing large work gloves, each player must pick up and unwrap ten pieces of wrapped gum lying flat on the floor, a table, or a tray. The winner is the one who picks up and unwraps the ten pieces first, or picks up the most in one minute.

Hot Air Champ: Give two–eight children identical balloons. Give a signal (clap hands, blow a whistle, etc.) six times. At each signal each child is to give a big puff into his/her balloon (see photo above). The winner is the one with the biggest balloon after the sixth puff. Of course, keeping the air in between puffs is part of the contest.

Saving Paper: Have identical shapes, paper, and pencils for each child. Instruct the participants to outline the shape as many times as possible on the paper — without overlapping. The winner is the one with the most complete outlines of the shape on the paper when time is called. You may make your shapes from cardboard or index cards using purchased stencils, a cookie cutter, or a simple coloring book drawing as a pattern. The shape may be related to your party theme or be an animal outline or a familiar cookie shape, such as a gingerbread man. Note that this can be a quiet game for two or three children to play as well as a contest for a larger group.

Doughnut Nibble.

Doughnut Nibble: Position a spring-loaded curtain rod securely in the top section of a doorway. Loop a piece of yarn through a doughnut. Tie the yarn to the curtain rod so that the doughnut is dangling chin high to the player. With hands behind his or her back, the player nibbles the doughnut until the doughnut falls from the yarn (see photo above). Someone should be standing by to catch the falling doughnut. If the floor needs protecting, cover it with newspaper, a throw rug, or a painters drop cloth. The winner is the player with the smallest piece of doughnut which fell from the yarn.

Macaroni String: Provide each player with a dull large-eyed needle, two–three feet of heavy thread, string, or yarn, and a supply of macaroni. Give three–five minutes for each player to string macaroni. The winner is the one with the largest count of macaroni on the string.

Life Saver Slide: Two players each hold one end of a three-foot string. One player puts his/her end of the string through a Life Saver.

Life Saver Slide.

The goal of the partners is to maneuver the Life Saver the entire length of the string without touching it (see photo above). If several pairs are working at the task, the winner is the pair which moves the Life Saver most quickly. If one pair at a time plays, they can try for the fastest time. Two children can race the clock trying to reduce their time with each try.

Too Hot to Hold: Players stand or sit in a circle and pass an object while the leader plays music, claps, or taps a drum. When the music or sound stops, the person with the "hot" article drops out of the circle. Many articles are appropriate to pass. Use something related to your party theme or use a stuffed animal, a ball, a potato, a cushion, or some other article durable enough to survive the handling.

Clean Your Room: List items that are commonly found in a child's room. Assign each child sitting in a circle to be one of the items. "It" stands in the center of the circle and calls out the names of two items found in a child's room. (It is a good idea to read the group the list of names given without indicating who has each name.) The players named the called items try to change seats while "It" tries to steal one of their seats. The player without a seat is always "It." If "It" says "Clean your room!" everyone must move and the player without a seat becomes "It." Consider giving a prize to the children who are not "It" during a round.

Examples of item names for Clean Your Room: bed, pillow, blanket, sheets, mirror, drawers, comb, brush, jeans, shirt, shoes, socks, car, doll, teddy bear, puzzle, book.

This classic game adapts to most themes. For example, use "Happy Birthday" to have everyone move, and name the players things often found at a birthday party — such as cake, candles, matches, ice cream, balloons, gifts, napkins, cups, prizes, punch, mothers, games, music.

String Broad Jump: Lay two strings at least six feet long on the ground or carpet about a foot apart. After each round of contestants completes jumping over both strings, they are moved an additional six inches apart. Any player who touches a string or fails to jump over both strings is eliminated. The winner is the player who makes the broadest jump.

Hankie Grab: Supply each player a man's handkerchief or a piece of cloth the size of a handkerchief. Supervise as they tuck one corner of the hankie into their back pocket or back waistband — leaving two-thirds of the handkerchief hanging loose. If no pocket or waistband is available, use masking tape to attach the hankie about where a pocket would be. At a signal, each player attempts to grab everyone else's hankie, while keeping his/her own safe. A player may not hold onto the handkerchief to prevent it from being taken. When the stop signal is given, the winner is the player who still has his/her hankie and has grabbed the most hankies belonging to others. When a player loses his/her hankie, he/she drops out of the game.

Clothing Snatch: Place articles of clothing such as hats, gloves, shirts, old large shoes, or housecoats, on a large table. For each round have one less article of clothing than you have players. Everyone marches around the table to music or clapping. When the music or

Sneak and Steal.

clapping stops, each person grabs an article of clothing and puts it on before the game leader can count slowly to ten. Everyone without one piece of clothing on at the end of the count drops out. The last round has two players and the one who manages to get on the last piece of clothing wins.

Sneak and Steal: A blindfolded "It" sits with an object in his/her lap. The other players, one at a time, attempt to sneak up and steal the object (see photo above). "It" may say "stop" at any time and point in the direction he/she thinks the thief is approaching. If "It" points in the correct direction, he/she remains "It." The player who actually grabs the object becomes "It." The object in "Its" lap can be anything that is close to the size of a shoe box. A gift-wrapped box would be good for a birthday party, or use a balloon, stuffed animal, ball, or pillow for other occasions. Encourage the children to be very quiet while they play this game.

Strainer Ball Toss: Supply each of two players with a strainer with a handle and one ball small enough to fit easily in the strainers. The players use the strainers — no hands — to toss and catch the ball. When the partners toss and catch the ball four times without the ball hitting the ground, each receives a prize. This activity works best outside. Each child needs room to move around, a strainer, and a partner to play with. Strainers often prove to be more durable than similar purchased games.

Circle and Keep: No player may leave the designated game area. Three players join hands and surround another player. The "caught" player may escape by ducking under but cannot break the hands of those surrounding him/her. The caught player joins the surrounding group and now four with joined hands surround another player, etc. The last three free players are the winners and begin the next game.

Flying Feathers: Divide the players into two or more groups of three–five members. Each group holds hands to form a close circle. Have a feather (a feather duster is a good source) for each group. At the leader's signal, the tallest person in each group drops the team's feather in the center of the circle and each team works together to keep their feather in the air by blowing it; no parts of their bodies may touch the feather. When one feather touches the ground all other groups win a point. Declare a winner when one group earns five points.

Back to Back Race: Pair the players and have them sit back to back with their elbows locking them together. Their task is to rise and walk to a goal and back and return to their sitting position without disconnecting their locked elbows.

Pinch the Pins: Place about 15 small, closed safety pins in a small bowl with uncooked long-grain rice. Blindfold the players and see how many pins they can locate and remove from the bowl of rice in one minute.

Balloon Stomp.

Balloon Stomp: Blow up a balloon for each participant, tie them, and attach each to the end of a four-foot string. Attach the other end of the four-foot string to the ankle of each player. The balloon must be allowed to float free and cannot be wound around the leg of the child to protect it. The object is for each player to stomp and pop other players' balloons while keeping his/her own safe (see photo above). The winner is the last player with a whole balloon attached to a leg. Be sure all players know the boundaries of where they are playing.

Domino Towers: Divide a large set of dominoes among the players who are seated around a table. Place one domino in the center of the table. Players take turns adding one of their dominoes to the stack to form a tower. The player who makes the stack fall drops out and the remaining players start a new round until only one player remains. This game is also excellent for only two players.

Bat the Balloon: See which child can first bat a big balloon to the ceiling three times without causing it to break. Then have a contest to see who can keep his/her balloon in the air the longest.

Shrinking Sack.

Stray Dog: Select four players to begin the game by being in the center of a circle of the other players. The four in the center line up single file and grab the back of the belt or waist of the child in front of them. Designate the first three in the line as neighborhood children and the last in the line as the "Stray Dog." The players making up the circle are trying to get rid of the Stray Dog by hitting it with a large, soft ball. The players in the circle may pass the ball or throw it at the Stray Dog. The three neighborhood children in the front of the line move around in a way that protects the Stray Dog from the ball. When someone hits the Stray Dog, the Stray Dog takes that player's place in the circle and the player who threw the ball takes the front position in the line of four in the center. The play begins again with a new Stray Dog.

Shrinking Sack: Open up a large paper grocery sack and stand it in the center of the game area. Each player takes a turn picking up the sack using only his/her mouth. Those who are unsuccessful or touch the floor/ground or who fall over are eliminated. After all have had a turn, prepare for the next round by cutting off the sack with scissors until the sack is half as tall. Continue the contest by cutting off half the sack for each round and eliminating those who fail. Give the prizes to those not eliminated when the sack is about two inches high.

4. Relay Fun

Relays are especially good for larger groups but will work with as few as six children with three on each team. If you have more than 20 players, consider having three or more teams doing each activity.

It is usually a good idea to do two to four relays in a row to take advantage of getting the group accustomed to the relay procedure. If the teams are unevenly matched in ability, mix the teams after each event so all have a chance to be a winner part of the time.

The winning team is the first team which has all of its members complete the assigned task.

Legs Alley: For each team, all members stand in a row, one behind the other, all facing forward with their legs firmly planted at least shoulder width apart, thus forming an alley of legs. The first person in each team is given a ball, bends forward at the waist, and throws the ball through his/her legs and the leg alley formed by the team members (see photo on page 59). After the ball clears the leg alley, the last person in the row picks up the ball, runs to the front of the line, takes the stance of the group, bends at the waist, and throws the ball down the alley; the last player in line runs to the head of the line, etc. The winning team is the one to first have the original player at the head of the line. The ball may not be touched or kicked or nudged by any player as it moves through the leg alley. If the ball does not make it through all the legs, it must be retrieved by the thrower who again takes the front of the line position, bends over and tries the throw again.

Gripped Knees Race: A goal line is established. One at a time, the members of each team walk or jump as quickly as possible to a goal line with a ball, balloon, or orange firmly gripped between their knees (see photo on page 59). If you have room, give all players a balloon and the winning team is the one which first has all the team members cross the finish line.

Left: **Legs Alley;** *right:* **Gripped Knees Race.**

Fill It Up: Give each team a container full of water, sand, popcorn, beans, rice, or marbles. Instruct them to take turns using a spoon to move what is in their container to an empty container at the goal line. The winning team is the one which has the most of the item moved into their container when time is called.

Push and Roll: Each team is provided a broom, a sponge mop, a ruler, or a yardstick to use—one at a time—to push and or roll a ball, a sock rolled into a ball, an orange, a lemon, a potato, a balloon, or an empty can from a beginning line to a finish line and back. After you choose your combination, try it out to be sure the push and roll will work, but not too easily.

Bag Lady Outfit: Each team receives a sack of assorted clothes. Be sure each team has the same number and similar articles of clothing. Team members take turns removing all the clothing from the sack, putting it all on, and then returning it to the sack for the next player (see photo on page 60).

Ball Kick: The members of each team take turns kicking their team's ball from the beginning line into an open box—lying on its

Bag Lady Outfit.

side — at the goal line. Only one foot, and no hands may touch the ball between the time it leaves the beginning line and is kicked into the box. After kicking the ball into the box, each player picks it up and positions it on the beginning line for the next team member.

Puzzle Relay: Buy two identical simple puzzles with 10–30 pieces. Lay out the puzzle pieces for each team on a flat surface. Team members go one at a time and fit one piece of the puzzle into place. The

Hoop Pass.

team which first completes their puzzle wins. Each player must locate and place his/her piece without advice or help.

Hoop Pass: Each team stands in a line. The first person in each line is given an embroidery hoop. The hoop is passed from child to child while shaking hands (see photo above). To win, the team must pass the hoop to the end of the line and back to the first person. If the hoop is maneuvered by other than shaking hands or is dropped, the hoop must start again with the first person in the line.

Hoola Hoop: The members of each team stand in a line with hands joined. The leader of each team receives a hoola hoop which must be passed along the line without the team breaking hands.

Candy Carry: Team members take turns carrying to a goal line and back a piece of wrapped candy (or a nut in the shell) on the toe of one shoe. If the candy/nut falls off the shoe, the player starts again from the beginning line.

Caterpillar Crawl.

Caterpillar Crawl: The members of each team kneel and grab the ankles of the person in front of them to form a caterpillar. While staying connected, the teams crawl to the goal together. The first caterpillar to completely cross the finish line is the winner.

No Props Needed: Some relays require no materials. For example, have the members of each team take turns going from a beginning spot to a goal line while (1) walking backwards, (2) hopping on one foot, (3) holding their ankles and walking with their knees locked or (4) while patting their head and rubbing their tummy.

Shoe Box Shuffle: The players take turns shuffling to a goal line and back with their feet in two large shoe boxes.

Balancing a Book: Set up duplicate barriers, such as chairs and or trash cans, between the beginning point and the goal line. The children on each team take turns walking the route while balancing a book on their head. They must go over or around the barriers.

Guiding the Blindfolded: For each team, designate one player or adult to blindfold each player and one player to be the team's guide by making a sound while each child is walking to the goal line blindfolded. The guide will remove the blindfold at the goal line. Each player will return the blindfold to the person doing the blindfolding. This game can be adapted to a theme by having the guides make some noise or say some phrase related to the party theme. The team guides at a birthday party might say over and over "Happy Birthday, [name of the birthday child]"; at a Halloween party the guides could moan like a ghost. Make sure the guide does not touch the blindfolded player.

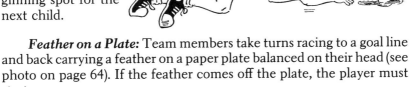

Feather Blow: Team members take turns blowing the team's feather from a beginning spot to a goal line on the floor or a long table (see illustration at right). After the feather reaches the goal line, each player returns it and places it at the beginning spot for the next child.

Feather on a Plate: Team members take turns racing to a goal line and back carrying a feather on a paper plate balanced on their head (see photo on page 64). If the feather comes off the plate, the player must start over.

Beans Balance: The children on each team take turns balancing three beans on a knife and walking to a goal line and back. If beans are dropped, the players must start again. Have extra beans on hand to replace any lost.

Egg Carry: One at a time each member of each team carries an egg in a spoon to a goal line and back. The egg should definitely be hard boiled if playing indoors, but it adds to the fun if you hint that it is raw.

Straw Carry: Prepare identical shapes from tissue wrapping paper or facial tissue for each team. Give each player a straw. The members of each team take turns picking up their team's tissue shape by sucking on their straw. Each player must use his/her straw to carry the shape to a goal line and back. A tissue dropped must be picked up with the straw only, no hands allowed. The tissue shapes may be related to the

Feather on a Plate.

party theme—ghosts for Halloween, hearts for Valentines, Christmas trees for Christmas, for example.

Through the Tunnel: Members of each team line up single file with each member spreading his/her legs apart. The last person in line on each team crawls between the legs of the players to the front (see photo on page 65), stands, and yells, "I'm through the tunnel!" The next person at the end of the line then crawls through the legs, stands and yells, "I'm through the tunnel!" Play continues until all the players on one team have made it through the tunnel.

Passing the Ring: Give each player an unsharpened pencil. Have the two teams line up single file. The first person on each team is given a ring—plastic rings that go on curtains are ideal. Each player passes the ring from his pencil to the pencil of the person behind him without using his free hand (see photo on page 65).

Buttons, Buttons!: Have each player select a large button from a bowl. Have the members of each team stand in a line. Give the first person on each team two pipe cleaners. The task for each player is to

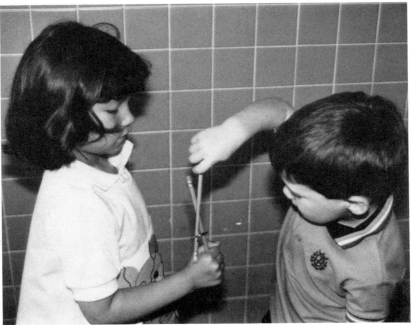

Top: Through the Tunnel; *bottom:* Passing the Ring.

thread his/her button on both pipe cleaners and then pass the pipe cleaners and button(s) to the next team member who will add his button, etc., to the end of the line. Allow younger children to work together getting the buttons on the pipe cleaners. Test all buttons to be sure they can be threaded on the pipe cleaners.

Sock Gloves: Give each team a pair of socks to use for gloves and a sack of wrapped candy. Each team member's task is to put a sock on each hand, take a piece of candy from the bag, unwrap the candy and put it in his/her mouth, and then pass the sack and the socks to the next team member.

Note: For more relay ideas consider the activities in the Skill Challenges chapter of this book; many of them will adapt easily to relays.

5. Making Something

When "making something" there will be some mess, so be prepared to clean up the area after the children's original creations are rescued for display or use. Consider preparing the area where children will be working by covering the floor and or table with old newspapers, a paint drop cloth, or an old shower curtain. You may want to plan several projects to take advantage of having the area prepared.

Show the children a sample of the project they will be doing, but stress that theirs will not look just like yours.

Divide the supplies and materials among the group, being sure all know which items must be shared. Don't forget supplies for cleaning up.

Be sure each child's name is placed somewhere on his project after it is completed.

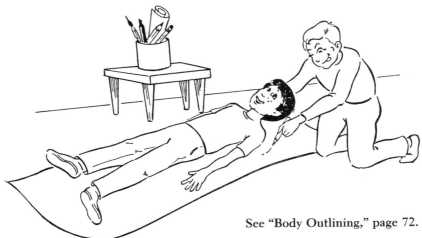

See "Body Outlining," page 72.

Story Pictures: Provide large pieces of drawing paper, pencils, colors, markers, stencils of letters and or shapes, and objects which can be drawn around for basic shapes such as coins, lids, small rulers, plastic animals and people. With these materials, each child creates a picture, colors it, and tells a story about what is happening in the picture.

Chef Time: Put an apron or an old, big shirt on everyone and cook one thing or several. Beginning with pizza mix, make individual pizzas; from pre-made dough, roll out, cut, bake and decorate sugar cookies; layer two flavors of instant pudding in clear plastic cups and decorate the top with chocolate chips or nuts; or make popcorn balls. These are just a few of the possibilities. Visit the library and check out a children's cookbook for ideas. Some ribbon awards related to the looks and taste of the items cooked can add to the fun. The products may be eaten and or prepared to use as gifts for parents.

Decorating Cloth Items: Provide each child with a cloth object to decorate. Although you may use items in light colors, white may be your best color choice. The objects to decorate may be a T-shirt, a sweat shirt, a place mat, an apron, a handkerchief, a dishcloth, a pillowcase, a cover for a cushion, a dresser scarf, a neck or head scarf,

Decorated tote bags.

a tote bag (see photo on page 68), a glasses case, a cloth-covered button, or any other item of plain material which lends itself to being decorated. Encourage each child to practice the picture or design he/she decides to use on paper, using a pencil; then provide fabric paint in tubes or paints and brushes to use to decorate the cloth object. The work should be done on a firm surface, such as a table or floor. Cover the work area with a thick layer of newspapers, a paint drop cloth, or an old shower curtain. Make some samples for the children to see. For the children who have trouble planning a decoration, suggest using their name or From *[the name of their town or state]*. A coloring book with simple pictures or a stencil set will also provide ideas. Don't forget to prepare a place for the items to be laid until the paint dries.

Puppets: Make puppets to act out a familiar story or nursery rhyme or have the children make up a story to tell with puppets. Puppets can be made from socks, sleeves from old clothes, fingers from old gloves, pan scratchers attached to the tops of large paper or plastic cups, two paper plates (stapled, glued, or sewn together), lunch bags, spoons, paper dolls, or pictures from coloring books mounted on pieces of cardboard and attached to a stick (see photos on page 70). Be sure and allow adequate time if you plan to make puppets and use them to tell a story. This one activity can be an entire party with the puppet show as the ending event. Chapter 8 has story ideas for puppet shows.

Balloon People/Animals: Turn balloons into people or animals by decorating them with felt-tip markers, tempera paint, brushes, colored paper, fabric scraps, glitter, glue, tape, ribbons, yarn, buttons, and such. Cardboard feet providing a slit for the tied end of the balloon will allow the people/animals to stand on their own (see photo on page 71). Long thin balloons can be twisted into shapes before decorations are added. Remember that each person or animal created deserves a name!

Bottle Vases/Candleholders: Decorate slim bottles with shapes cut from contact paper to make attractive bud vases or candleholders. Consider any bottle that is tall and slim and can be cleaned of labels. Your kitchen should offer several possibilities. Soda bottles will give you a quick supply.

Cookie Sheet Painting: Use poster paints to create a picture or design on a cookie sheet.

Puppets.

Balloon Animals.

Vegetable Dolls: Use construction paper, toothpicks, raisins, buttons, yarn, cotton, glue, ribbons, scraps of material, and other common items to turn vegetables or a combination of vegetables (squash, potatoes, eggplant, turnips, carrots, for example) into dolls (see photo, right). These dolls are interesting for the children to make but can be played with or used as decorations for only a day or two before they will begin to spoil.

Badges: Cut circles of thin cardboard, tape a safety pin to the back, and decorate them. The badges can be used as name tags, team identification tags, or simply as decorations. For older children, have a list of clever sayings to suggest for decorations.

Body Outline: Each child lies on a large sheet of paper while someone draws around him/her to create a life-sized outline. Then the child can use markers, crayons, or paints to fill in features and clothes on his/her outline. A large wall is great for displaying the outlines until they are taken home.

Rock Paperweights: Collect big smooth pebbles and rocks— perhaps from a visit to a river, ocean, or a rock shop. Allow the children to use poster paints to create a design or picture on the rocks (see photo below). When the works of art are dry, you may want to have the children apply varnish to preserve the picture and make it shine. The paperweights make nice gifts to give parents, grandparents, and teachers.

Rock paperweights.

Puzzles: Use rubber cement to glue a picture from a magazine to light cardboard. On the back of the cardboard draw lines and curves similar to purchased puzzles. Cut along the drawn lines. Spend some time exchanging and playing with the puzzles. You might also want to make puzzles from pictures you've laminated at a school supply store or from enlarged photographs. To keep from mixing up the puzzles, have the children write their name on the back of each piece of the puzzle they made. Provide an envelope, lunch sack, or plastic sack to use to take the puzzles home. Be sure the child's name is on the envelope or sack.

Pictures Prop: Help each child create a picture prop for instamatic pictures by drawing a hat, hair, collar or scarf on a poster board around a cut-out circle the size of a child's face. After the prop is finished, take an instamatic picture with the child's face surrounded by the drawing on the poster. A clown, a cowboy, batman, a lady with elaborate curled hair, and a witch are examples of props children might like to do.

Bean Bags: Stuff the end of an old or odd sock with dried beans or corn and sew or staple the end together. Provide yarn, felt, fabric scraps, markers, glue, and such for decorating the bean bags. After the bags are finished, play a game of bean bag toss between players or see who is the most accurate throwing their bag into an empty container. If you do not have old socks, make the bean bags out of strong material sewed on a sewing machine on three sides. Sew or staple the fourth side after the bags are decorated and stuffed.

Torn Shape Art: Give each child a piece of construction paper. Have them each tear out three "interesting" shapes. After they all have their torn shapes, provide clean paper, tape or glue, and crayons or markers. Instruct everyone to use all of their shapes as part of an animal, person, thing, or scene. They may add to their shapes only by drawing with their crayons or markers. After the pictures are finished, the creator should show the work of art and tell its title/name. Let the other players suggest other possible titles or names.

A Color Lesson Book: Have two or three children work together to make a color lesson book. Make a list of the most common colors. Provide old magazines, safe scissors, glue, yarn, markers, crayons, and a supply of punched paper. The groups find each color on your list in one of the old magazines and cut out a piece. The piece is glued to a sheet

Shoe Box Slide.

of punched paper and the name of the color printed under it. When the group has a page for each color on the list, they use yarn to tie the punched sheets together to form a color lesson book. Donate the books to a church nursery, nursery school or a teacher of young children.

Shoe Box Slide: Make a slide from shoe boxes or shoe box lids attached to each other with staples or tape. You may want to cover the slide with contact paper and or decorate its sides. The slide in the picture (see above) is shoebox lids attached with wide, clear tape made for taping parcels to mail. Place one end of the slide on a chair with the landing spot on the floor or lay the slide across the bottom steps of a stairway. Cars, dolls, blocks and the like all love to slide. Two of them might want to "race" to the bottom.

Patterns on Containers: Create patterns by attaching beans, corn, and or different sizes of macaroni to a container with glue. After the glue sets, you may want to spray-paint the container. Cookie and candy tins, coffee cans, nut cans, or flowerpots will work well with this activity.

Spoon Family: Use markers to draw faces on the back of wooden and cooking spoons of various sizes. Glue on paper hats and clothes and create a family (see photo below). When the family is complete, the creator can tell a story about them or use them as puppets.

Spoon Family.

Modern Sculptures: Collect scraps of lace, rickrack, ribbon, wood, wooden beads, corks, plastic spoons/knives/forks, pretty rocks, shells, macaroni, colored cotton balls, buttons, empty cans, small jars, ice cream sticks, straws, glitter, old or broken jewelry, and other common items, and invite the children to create an original modern sculpture with a title.

Silhouette Pictures: In a dark area, set up a floodlight or a trouble light so that the shadow of a child seated sideways in front of the light will reflect on a sheet of drawing paper on a wall or easel behind the seat. Trace around the shadow of the head and neck and then give each child his/her silhouette to make a self-portrait or make a solid colored silhouette to glue on a sheet of paper.

Churning Butter: Fill baby food jars, or other small containers with tight-fitting lids, half full of heavy cream. Have the children shake them until they make butter. Let them spread their butter on a cracker and eat it. Test your cream and jar churns to be sure they will make butter in a reasonable length of time. Having partners working with one jar is a good idea since this can be tiring if a child does it alone.

Crocheting: Teach the children to crochet. They might make a dishrag for Mom, a shawl for a doll, a blanket for a baby bed, a belt, or headband. This might be a project that they could finish at home. Most projects would take longer than your average party.

Decorated Light Switches: Use acrylic paint and a small brush to paint a design, a picture and or a name on a light switch plate (see photo on page 77) which can easily be installed in the child's room.

Sponge Boats: Cut sponges into various shapes with scissors. Allow the children to use a water-resistant glue to put the shapes together to form boats which can be played with in the tub or pool (see photo on page 77).

Play Dough: Most children love play dough. Make some sample items, cover the child with an old shirt, protect the working surface and surrounding area with a plastic tablecloth and drop cloth and watch the fun. If you don't have purchased dough on hand, try making some. For each color desired: Mix 2 cups of floor, 1 cup of salt, 4 tablespoons of oil and then add colored water—a little at a time—until the mixture is

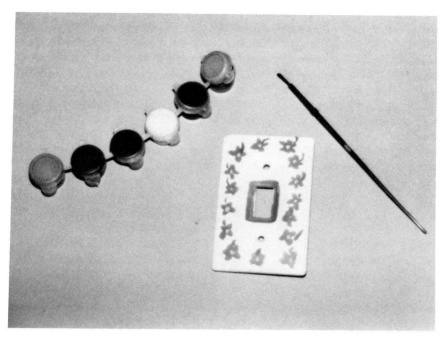

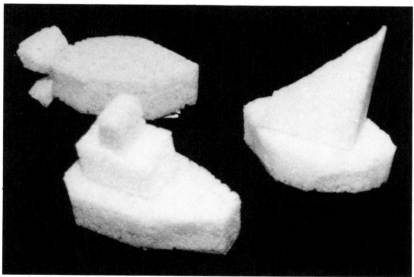

Top: Decorated light switches; *bottom:* Sponge boats.

Baked salt dough octopus.

thick and easy to handle. Store the clay in an airtight container between uses.

Salt Dough: To produce shapes which can be painted later, make dough by mixing 1 cup of salt, 2 cups of flour, ¾ cup of water and 2 tablespoons of salad oil. Have the child/children form the dough into a desired shape and then bake it in the oven at 350 degrees until it is lightly browned. Let the sculpture cool before decorating it with acrylic paints.

6. Finding Things

Finding something delights the heart of a child. Usually this type of activity calls for some advanced planning and preparation by the person in charge, but the results are well worth the effort.

Stringing It Together: Form several teams with four–eight members each, select a leader for each group, and assign each group a sound. The assigned sounds can be related to a party theme or something selected at random, like the sounds of different animals or musical instruments or lines from different nursery rhymes. The members of each team find pieces of string or yarn of various lengths hidden around the room or yard, stand in front of the string and make the sound assigned to their team; the team leader comes to collect the string. The team members cannot touch or point to the string and the team leader cannot pick up a string unless a team member is making their sound by it. After the strings are all found, or time is called, each team lays their strings end to end and the winner is the team with the longest line of string.

Tracking the Weird Beast: Just before the party starts, an adult uses something to make unusual tracks for the children to follow (see illustration below). A piece of cardboard can be used to make a stencil

Making weird beast tracks.

of an unusual track and the stencil filled in with flour, powdered sugar, glitter, or spray paint, depending on how many tracks are to be made and where they will be made. This idea will, of course, work best in a field, forest path, or park. Long before the end of the trail is reached, the beast should have a name made up by the trackers. A picnic basket or package of food left by the beast where the trail disappears would be a nice ending for the adventure.

Building a Collection: Collecting and displaying stamps or coins make a great hobby for children and provide many hours of pleasure, but some less traditional items can be just as much fun to collect. Suggest some of the following for collections: labels from fruits; empty soda cans or bottles — one of each kind; buttons of a certain color or size; buttons with slogans; ticket stubs; advertisements for movies you've seen; key chains; whistles; candy bar wrappers; motel/hotel soap; advertising pencils; advertising pens; refrigerator magnets; picture postcards with a common theme (famous people/old houses/animals); earrings — one of a kind; marbles of different colors/designs; lollipops/suckers; thimbles; maps; restaurant place mats; napkin rings; handkerchiefs; small mirrors; ball caps; miniature cars; fashion doll hats.

Ticking Timer: An adult or selected child hides a ticking kitchen timer — set to go off in five minutes. The players quietly enter the area where the timer is hidden and see who can locate it first. The one who finds the timer hides it for the next search.

Shoe Scramble: All children remove their shoes and place them in a pile in the center of a circle formed by the children. The leader mixes the shoes so mates are not together. At the leader's signal, all rush to find their own shoes and get them on. The winner is the first player to report to a specified spot with both of his/her shoes completely on. (They do not have to be fastened.) This is an old game, but one children love. A unique twist is to blindfold all children and then have them locate and put on what they believe to be their own shoes.

Small Item Hunt: In the tradition of the Easter egg hunt, hide small plastic objects outside for the children to find. Let the child who finds the most objects help hide the objects for a second round. Give prizes for the most items found and for designated "special" pieces.

Matching Yarn by Size: From one color of yarn, cut ten pieces of yarn 1 inch long, ten pieces of yarn 2 inches long, ten pieces of yarn 3 inches long, etc. — until you have a set of ten yarn pieces for each child. Hide nine pieces of each set around the playing area. Place all of the pieces you still have — one of each set — in a container and have each player select one of the pieces. At a signal, each player tries to find the nine hidden pieces which match his/her one. The first child to deliver all ten pieces which are the same length to the leader earns a prize. If you decide to play more than once, let the winner of each

round join in the hiding of the pieces. This makes hiding faster and in-
sures that more children earn a prize.

Numbered Items: Hide ten different small objects in a large game
area. This is a good activity for a school or church building or a park.
By each item, place a number 1-10 which can be easily read by the
searchers. Make a list of the hidden items (not in the order numbered)
for each player and provide each with a pencil. The winner is the
searcher who first gives the leader a list with the correct number written by each item. Be sure the hidden objects are represented by words
the children can read. Read the list with them before they begin searching. Small plastic toys work well for this activity. One sack of plastic
animals may provide most of the ten items. Other items to hide could
be a small car, doll, ball, box, ribbon, pencil, crayon, toothbrush, shoe,
or belt.

Flashlight Tag: Flashlight Tag works best in a large definite area
which can be made very dark. "It" leaves the area while everyone hides.
The leader turns out the lights, gives "It" a flashlight, and turns him/
her loose to find the hidden players by shining his/her flashlight on
them. The hidden players may move around if they wish. The last person tagged becomes "It" for the next round. It is necessary to remove
dangerous and breakable items from the area before the game and to
have good adult supervision. Under the right circumstances, children
will want to play this game over and over.

Find the Drummer: Outside, in a big yard or park area, give one
player a drum or tambourine to beat and have him/her hide while
other players hide their eyes. The hidden drummer then softly beats
the drum every few seconds until someone finds him/her. Let the person who first finds the drummer be "It" the next round.

Any noisemaker can be substituted for the drum. This game is
good inside for young children with the one(s) looking for the sound
blindfolded. The room for this activity should be fairly uncluttered. An
adult should watch the blindfolded child/children closely to prevent
injury.

Things That Don't Belong: In a specific area, have the children
walk around collecting things that don't belong there. In a living room
or family room, the things that don't belong might be a leaf, a rock, a
piece of grass, a toothbrush, toothpaste, a piece of toilet paper, a

dishrag, a bottle of cologne, a hammer, a wrench. Outside, the things that don't belong might be a clock, a pen, a handkerchief, a lunch box, a sock, a brush, birthday candles, a salt shaker, a bottle of ketchup, a basket, a tape measure, a spool of thread (see photo on page 84). There are many possibilities for things that don't belong. Just be prepared to explain why they don't belong, if some of the children are confused by the game.

Lost Lamb: One player becomes the Lost Lamb with a bell hanging around his/her neck. All other players are blindfolded and try to catch the Lost Lamb who must stay within the playing area. The person who catches the Lost Lamb trades places with him/her for the next round.

Bus Ride: Take the children on a bus ride in a city. During the ride they will watch for specific things you tell them to watch for or have written on a piece of paper. You will, of course, go on the ride yourself before the trip and make your list of items to find. The planning ride will also let you note times and any possible problems.

Treasure Hunt: Treasure hunts sometimes seem to be too much trouble to plan and set up, but they can be arranged in a minimum of time if you begin by planning where you want to hide the clues and then write the clues to fit the hiding places. I favor placing the clues all in envelopes and writing Clue 1, Clue 2, etc., on the outside of the envelopes. Have a clue envelope for each player or team at each location. The prize(s) can be with the last clue or the last clue can provide the secret word or phrase which can be told to the leader in exchange for the prize. The following clues will adapt to many locations and give examples of the kind you can write.

Clue 1 (Given at the beginning)
You I do not wish to bore,
But have you looked behind the door?

Clue 2 (Behind a door)
Although the cover is not red,
You should search under the bed.

Clue 3 (Under a bed)
Search and find the right black shoe,
And you will find a clue or two.

Things That Don't Belong.

Clue 4 (Under or in a right black shoe)
Can you find soda cans in a row?
A clue near them tells you where to go.

Clue 5 (Near soda cans in a row)
Find a jacket hanging in view,
Inside the pocket is a clue for you.

Clue 6 (In a jacket pocket)
Taped beneath a chair seat,
Is as good a clue as you need to meet.

Clue 7 (Under a chair)
Find a magazine on a table fast,
Inside is a clue, but not your last.

Clue 8 (Inside a magazine)
Look for a sweet Teddy,
He has a clue for you when you're ready.

Clue 9 (With a teddy bear)
Look for a small ugly rug,
Its clue is better than if you dug.

Clue 10 (Under a rug)
The clue that you'll find under a box,
Is so much fun it'll blow your socks.

Last Clue (Under a box)
Do not despair,
You're almost there!
Go tell the leader that you are "pint size,"
And for those words receive a prize.

Other sample last clues:

This is your treasure!
Take one sack,
And put the others back.

You've won — your team's the best,
Take the prizes in this treasure chest.

Photo Scavenger Hunt: Go seeking things on a list for the purpose of taking a picture. Let older children bring a camera or supply teams with one to share. With younger children, have an adult take a picture of the children with each item. An instamatic camera is good but having to wait to see the pictures will make fun for another day. A zoo, park, and an airport are a few of the places that would be good hunting grounds.

If you know someone with a farm, ask if you can bring children to visit them. You might even be able to arrange to find a horse and end the adventure with a horseback ride for each child.

7. Thinking Games

These games and activities encourage thinking and or creativity from children. If you think differences due to age or natural ability will make some players uncomfortable, select the activities which stress teamwork. Be quick to praise and show genuine pleasure in response to their efforts.

Numbers Up: Form teams of five–ten children. When there are not enough children for teams, let the group play together to race the stopwatch or timer and provide a treat when they "beat the clock" a specified number of times.

Give each team a set of large numbers — 0–9 — drawn on ten sheets of construction paper. Each team member must be responsible for a number; if there are less than ten children, one or more will have a number for each hand. The leader calls a number — such as 1439 — and each team competes to be first to line up their players with those numbers in the proper order for the leader to read the number called. The numbers called must use each number only once. If the numbers become too simple to form, try asking for the answers to math problems such as $15 \times 10 - 4$ to have the players form 146 with their numbers.

Animal Charades: Print the names of animals familiar to children on slips of paper, fold the slips, and place them in a container. The players take turns selecting a slip and acting like the animal written on the slip (see photo on page 87). The actor must make no sounds but may use gestures to encourage or discourage those guessing. Allow each player two minutes to act like his/her animal. The first person to guess the animal being portrayed wins a prize. If someone guesses the animal, the actor also wins a prize. For a longer session, give points instead of prizes and the winner is the one with the most points. If the children are too young to read the name of the animal, the person leading the activity should take the child aside after he/she draws a slip

86

Animal Charades.

and tell him/her the animal and perhaps give some hints on how to act like the animal.

Suggestions for animals to use: dog, cat, horse, bull, frog, duck, goat, chicken, pig, lion, seal, mouse, squirrel, snake, alligator, ostrich, monkey, rabbit, turtle, elephant, bear.

What Is Missing?: A player is selected, taken from the room, removes and hides some article of clothing, and returns to the game area. The other children must guess what is missing. The child that guesses correctly becomes "It" for the next round. Be sure and change games just before the children have everyone's clothing memorized.

Backward Spelling Bee: Have players take turns spelling words backwards. If the word is spelled correctly—in reverse order—within 30 seconds a prize or a point is earned. A set of flashcards at an appropriate level of difficulty is a good source of words or ask a teacher for a word list. The words should be easy for the players to spell. Even dog, cat, toy, bus, car, etc., will produce a fun game session. This game can also be played in teams with the team members helping each other. The time limit will add to the excitement.

What Is It?: Number brown grocery bags from 1 to 10 and place a different item in each bag. The leader has each player, in turn, close his/her eyes and carefully feel the item in the sack. After feeling the item, the leader reminds the players of the sack's number. After all have felt all the items, the leader challenges the children, as a group, to identify all ten items by sack number. If they can, all receive a prize. If they can't, you may want to switch the items around and give them a second chance.

Mystery Friend: Have each child bring a stuffed toy in a sack to the party. One at a time, take the toys out of the sacks and have the children guess which player brought the toy/friend being displayed. All who guess correctly receive a prize. The owner will, of course, guess correctly; if no one else guesses correctly, the owner of the toy will receive an extra prize. Do not return the mystery friends until the end of the game or the end of the party. Part of the thinking is remembering who has already been identified as the owner of one of the toys.

Mystery Artist: Give everyone identical paper and pencil, pen, marker, or crayon. Instruct them to draw a dog (change the assignment to fit a theme) without letting anyone see their picture. Collect all pictures and mix their order. Use a marker to write a different number in the corner of each work of art. On paper and pencil given to each player, have each child guess who drew each picture by matching the name of an artist to one of the numbers on the pictures. Learn the answer for each number and give a prize to the child with the most correct guesses.

Answer Yes or No: A player thinks of a specific item in the chosen category. The other players ask questions which require only a yes or no answer—until they guess the correct answer. This is a good game for adults to play with one or two children, as well as a fun game for several children. It is an effective way to encourage logical thinking and to increase knowledge. Try the following categories: I am thinking of . . . an animal, an object in this room/car, a toy I own, a piece of clothing, a relative, or a food. There are many possibilities!

Acting Out Nursery Rhymes: Divide the children into teams with two to four members. The group plans how to act out a nursery rhyme which is assigned to them. Everyone in the group must have some part of the presentation. An adult should help each team and it is important to have simple props available for some nursery rhymes. For example, a bucket/pail is definitely helpful when acting out Jack and Jill. A hockey stick can be used as Little Bo Peep's staff. When a nursery rhyme is acted out (no words), the audience tries to guess which one is being performed.

A variation of this activity is to have the team act out what they think the people in the nursery rhyme did right after the rhyme ended. For example: What did Jack and Jill do after their tumble? Did they go to the hospital? Did they blame each other for the fall? Did mother scold them for getting dirty or losing the water? In this case, the audience is told the name of the nursery rhyme and they try to guess from the acting what the characters did.

Which Is False?: Each child tells four personal facts about himself/herself; three facts must be true and one must be false. The other children try to guess which fact is false. Provide a couple of sample rounds. The following is an example. (1) I was born in St. Louis. (2) I have one sister. (3) My mother's name is Susan. (4) I am in the third grade. Three of the facts should be true and the fourth one false. In this case, the third fact may be false because the name of the mother of the player is Brenda, not Susan. This game is for children who are at least eight years old.

Under the Sheet: This activity works best when you have 12 or more children together. Divide the group in half and play the game in two rooms with an adult supervising each group. Select a child from each room, take them to a third room, cover them both completely with a large sheet, and then assist a sheeted child into each room. With this method, the players will not know whether the child under the sheet is the player taken from their group or a member of the group playing in the other room. The players question the child hidden by the sheet, trying to learn his/her identity (see photo on page 90). The person under the sheet must answer the questions without telling a lie — some evTasion is permissible, as is disguising the voice.

Purchasing Price: Cut out of advertisements or old catalog pictures of about 10 to 20 items children might want to purchase. Be sure

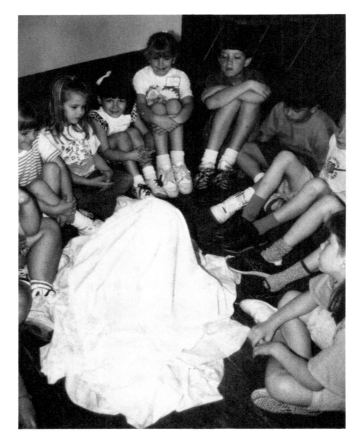

Under the Sheet.

and record the price of the items for your answer sheet. Tape each item
to the top third of a sheet of paper. Provide each child with a pencil.
Pass the papers with the pictures around the group and have each
player write his/her first name on the paper and indicate how much
they think the item costs (see photo on page 91). Have all papers passed
at the same time and do not start all of the sheets with the same player.
For each item, provide a prize for the one who lists the price closest
to the value of the item, without going over. Be sure everyone understands that your answer sheet is the final authority for the value of the
items. Most children need to be eight years or older to enjoy this activity.

Purchasing Price.

Jelly Bean Flavors: Buy a large supply of gourmet jelly beans. Review with the children the various flavors of jelly beans you will be using for the game. Take turns blindfolding contestants, feeding them three jelly beans from your collection, and asking them to identify the flavor of each (see illustration on page 92). Correct identification earns a prize.

Who Am I?: "It" sits in a chair blindfolded. The leader points to another player who quietly goes to stand behind "It" and, in a disguised or silly voice, says, "Who am I?" "It" must guess the identity of the questioner in two tries or remain "It." If the person asking "Who am I" fools "It," a prize is given; if the identity is guessed, the questioner becomes "It." Select a new "It" after he/she fails to guess three people.

Jelly Bean Flavors.

Nursery Rhymes Guess: Secure a book which contains a collection of well known nursery rhymes. Your library is an excellent source. Gather the children around, give them a clue and have them guess, from the clue, which nursery rhyme you plan to read next. You may want to select your rhymes ahead of time and write out your clues. When someone guesses correctly give them a prize or a point and read the nursery rhyme to everyone while showing the accompanying picture(s). Then give another clue to the next nursery rhyme.

Sample clues:

There was a game of follow the leader. (Mary Had a Little Lamb)

Someone was giving away wool? (Baa, Baa Black Sheep)

A cow makes a flying trip. (Hey, Diddle, Diddle)

An animal is scared at one o'clock. (Hickory, Dickory, Dock)

He runs around in his nightgown. (Wee Willie Winkie)

This fellow may get burned. (Jack Be Nimble)

Birds sing for the king. (Sing a Song of Sixpence)

The first animal went shopping and the last one cried a lot. (This Little Pig)

Someone was put in a funny prison. (Peter, Peter, Pumpkin-Eater)

She needed to go to the grocery store. (Old Mother Hubbard)

Their paws are very cold for a while. (Three Little Kittens)

He took a nap instead of standing guard. (Little Boy Blue)

Do the Opposite: The leader calls out commands and the players do the opposite. If the leader said "sit down," players should stand up. If the leader said "smile," players should frown. If the leader said "kick your leg forward," players should kick a leg backwards.

Ransom Notes: Divide players into two teams. Supply each team with old newspapers, scissors, paper, and tape. The teams race to see who can first compose a ransom note for someone or something kidnapped—using only words cut from a newspaper. The note must be at least 10 words long and make sense (see photo below). Some words can be formed one letter at a time. Teams for this game need at least one or two older children or an adult to help.

Ransom Note.

Cloth-Wrapped Items: Wrap about 10 items individually in pieces of cloth — such as scarves, handkerchiefs, cloth napkins, or pillowcases — and pass them around for all players to feel. Players may not talk or discuss the item during the feeling time. After everyone has carefully felt each item, lay them all in the center of the group. Provide pencil and paper and have the children list the items they think are wrapped in each cloth. Then hold up each item, listen to the various guesses of the players, and then unwrap the item to see if the guesses are correct. The child with the most correct items listed on their paper wins a prize. If you are playing with younger children, let them all guess together after all have felt each item or use fewer items.

Cartoon Captions: Give two to four children a cartoon or comic strip with the caption(s) missing. Have them make up what the characters are saying. Praise their efforts and then read them the caption(s) that came with the cartoon/comic strip. Books of cartoons and or comic strips written for children are the easiest source for this game, but newspapers also have suitable material.

Story/Skit Starters: Provide a sack of objects and ask the children to do a skit using the items in the sack or to tell a story involving each object in the sack. Almost any item can be woven into a story or skit. The following are some examples: a piece of fruit, a hat, a toy, a book, a flashlight, a tool, a cushion, a bell, a small box, a pencil. If the children have trouble getting started, share the following sample story:

> A package arrived for Billy one day. He opened it and found his Uncle Joe had sent him a *flashlight,* a *small shovel,* and a *small box* with the lid taped shut. He opened the box and inside was a letter saying Billy should go to the back of his school at midnight and dig up the rose bush by the cafeteria door. That night at 11:30, Billy put his lucky *hat* on his head and an *apple* in his pocket in case he was gone a long time. He carried a *sack* holding the shovel and used the flashlight to see where he was going. Even with the flashlight, he stumbled over a *cushion* and a *toy truck* as he slipped quietly across the living room. At school he dug up the rosebush and found a metal box containing a *book.* At midnight he heard a *bell* ringing close by. Billy was so scared he threw everything in his sack and ran all the way home. When he looked at the book he had found, it had a note attached. The note said "Happy Birthday,

Billy." I thought you'd like this book more if it was part of an adventure. Billy found a *pencil* so he could write Uncle Joe and say "Thank you."

Have two or three sacks of items ready in case the children want to create more than one skit or story. For younger children, base the skit/story on only three or four items.

Listening Test: Record a variety of sounds and have the children guess what they are hearing. The guessing can be all together for fun or as teams for a contest. Sounds you might record are many, for example: balloon bursting, telephone ringing, toilet flushing, car horn, alarm clock, and brushing teeth.

Word Search Poster: Create a large word search game on poster paper or a large piece of wrapping paper. Challenge the children — as a group — to find all of your hidden words. Be sure and tell them how many words they need to locate. The words can be related to any category or theme. The puzzles/games are easy to create; simply fill in the words you want found and then fill in the rest of the grid areas at random. The following puzzles are examples using toys and words related to Halloween. If you use names, you may want to use the names of children attending the party.

B	F	H	O	R	S	E	R
A	M	B	O	O	K	J	P
T	I	I	A	C	P	U	U
W	C	K	Y	R	T	S	Z
D	A	E	N	A	B	A	Z
O	R	G	E	Y	A	I	L
L	W	U	O	O	L	L	E
L	V	X	M	N	L	O	Q

Toys:

horse
book
bat
doll
car
Barbie
wagon
bike
crayon
ball
puzzle
drum

H	A	B	R	O	O	M	S
B	A	T	R	E	A	T	P
A	T	U	E	H	T	O	U
P	G	R	N	E	W	U	M
P	H	W	I	T	C	H	P
L	O	I	I	C	E	J	K
E	S	T	R	E	K	D	I
S	T	G	O	B	L	I	N

Halloween Words:

broom
apples
bat
ghost
witch
trick
goblin
haunted
pumpkin
treat

Solutions to puzzles:

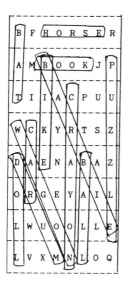

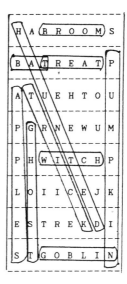

8. The Show Must Go On

Children love to plan and practice to perform for an audience. They can be divided into teams of any number and given instructions on what they are to plan and or practice. A single "act" may be prepared or a longer "program" made up of several "acts" planned. The performance can be for the larger group of children after everyone has practiced or for adults at a later time. Video cameras are wonderful for giving a special air of importance to the proceedings and for letting the children enjoy seeing themselves on television.

The following ideas will produce a single act and any combination of them will create a program to climax the fun of preparing to perform.

These activities can also be part of a theme party.

Actors and Actresses: Provide a costume and dress-up box, and perhaps some makeup, and have the children put together costumes and practice a short skit or play to perform (see photo on page 98). The children may choose to act out a nursery rhyme, a children's story such as *Cinderella* or *Jack and the Beanstalk,* or a story they made up. The following are idea starters for a skit or short play.

> Fishing adventures
> Disasters at a tea party
> A birthday party for two-year-olds
> The monkey who ran away from the zoo
> Hiding a stray pet from Mom and Dad

Put items like these in your costume box:

scarves	boots
hats	high heel shoes
gloves	ribbons
bandannas	yarn

97

Going to a tea party.

neckties
purses/billfolds
cloaks (full skirts make good
   cloaks)
walking canes
play dishes
safety pins
colored sheets
old tablecloths
curtains
costume jewelry

tote bags
small suitcases
shawls
yardsticks
construction paper
scissors
tape
markers
colorful lengths of material
staplers

Add things needed for ideas you plan to suggest. For example: fishing poles for a fishing adventure, a stuffed monkey for the escape from the zoo idea, etc.

Ending of a drill team routine.

Drill Team Routines: The children do a planned set of movements in unison and or movements which follow each other in a planned order. Costumes or props may be provided to add to the fun. Taped or live music might be appropriate or have someone provide a drum or tambourine beat to move by. A story may be illustrated by the drill.

To help design the movements for the routines, the adult leader and or the children can get started by thinking of or watching pom-pom groups, cheerleaders, dance routines (watch a variety show on television or go to a local dance recital), aerobic classes, or exercise class movements. Small children might do animal sounds and motions in unison such as walking like a duck, swinging arms like an elephant's trunk, or scratching like a monkey. A rifle team–type drill, acting out motions common to a sport, moving as you would doing household chores (sweeping, dusting, cooking), and getting ready for school are only a few of the possibilities for a drill team routine.

Costumes and props should be simple. They may include scarves around the head and black eye patches for pirates; matching T-shirts; white shirts for everyone; similar type hats such as ball caps or straw hats; beach towels; brooms, yardsticks, or any item which can be part of all or some of the drill movements; or pom-poms may be made from crepe paper or yarn.

Dance Routine: Have a dance teacher or an advanced dance student teach the children a simple dance routine which they can perform wearing simple costumes.

Two-Person Jokes: Partners prepare to tell jokes in vaudeville style. Almost any joke can be made into a two-person joke. For example, 1st Person: Why did the chicken cross the road? 2nd Person: I don't know, why did it? 1st Person: To get to the other side. Use the jokes the children know and a good children's joke book from the library or a bookstore for material.

Children's Band: Form a children's band to accompany taped music or someone playing a piano. Band instruments can be real ones or the children can use sauce pan lids for cymbals, pans and wooden spoons or sticks for drums, two wooden spoons for rhythm sticks, rattles made of beans in a tin can or covered soap dish. Have a conductor to help keep everyone in time with the music. This could be a marching band.

Flannel Board Stories: Cover a large board or piece of heavy cardboard with a piece of flannel material. Glue felt or sandpaper to the back of pictures from magazines, coloring books, or paper dolls. Have the children make up and tell a story while using the flannel board to illustrate the story or introduce the characters (see photo below).

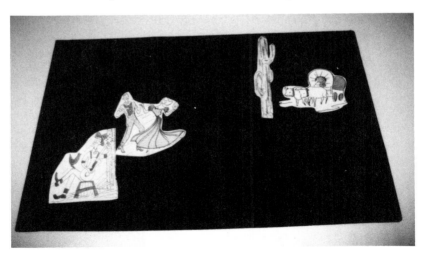

Flannel Board Stories.

Songs and Motions: Obtain a children's songbook—from a teacher, the library, or a music or bookstore. Select songs with words which fit with motions and or sounds. Have the children practice for a performance. The children may add motions to a song such as the traditional rowing motions to "Row, Row, Row Your Boat" or act like the animals in "Old MacDonald Had a Farm" or substitute a "toot-toot" for the word "train" in a song. Ask the children for suggestions of motions and sounds to use, but be ready with your own ideas to get them started.

Tape Recorder Fun: Tape recorders are reasonably priced and can be used to let one or more children tape a favorite story using different voices and sound effects. Any favorite story is a possibility; the classics like "The Three Little Pigs," "Red Riding Hood," or "Goldilocks" are excellent choices since the children will know the stories. If they want to, let them rearrange events, add new characters, or even change the ending.

Tape recorders are also fun for pretend news reporter interviews. An adult or older child plays a reporter and asks the other children their opinion or information on some topic. The reporter might ask—

What do you like best about school?
If I could give you any pet you want, what would you ask for? Why?
What would I find if I looked under your bed?
What rewards do you sometimes get for being very, very good?

Don't fail to leave adequate time for the climax of a tape recorder activity—playing back the created tape.

Verses to the Beat: Recite individually or in small groups nursery rhymes or children's poems to the beat of a drum or piano chord or the shaking of a tin can of beans. Keep the beat of the drum, piano, or can in a steady rhythm and have the children fit the words to the beat. A good rhythm for this activity is *slow, slow, fast, fast, fast* repeated over and over.

Puppet Shows: Use puppets to act out nursery rhymes, children's stories or some assigned event like

Puppet Shows.

- the first day of school
- a trip to the dentist
- trick-or-treating
- being naughty
- having the chicken pox
- helping mom or dad
- visiting grandparents
- a birthday party
- going to a movie
- going skating on a pond

See Chapter 5 for suggestions on making puppets.

9. Pool Activities

Sometimes planned activities are desirable for children playing in a pool—large or small—to calm down the action or to fight boredom.

Following Commands: Organize teams of three to five participants. The leader gives an instruction, says "GO," and the first team to have all members following the command wins 10 points. Commands can be right foot out of the water, float on your back, hold your nose and pat your head, put your right hand behind your head and your left hand on your right knee, and others.

Boat Race: Have a race across the pool with identical, sturdy plastic boats which can be moved *only* by making waves behind them (see illustration below). The boats cannot be touched by any part of the body or any object.

Boat Race.

103

Sponge Shapes.

Water Pistol Tag: "It" gets other players out of the game by hitting them with water shot from a water pistol. For older children supply targets made of small slick paper plates hung around their necks with yarn. The last person to be tagged becomes the next "It." If being "It" becomes too popular, take turns seeing how many people can be tagged with a water pistol spray in a two-minute period of time.

Sponge Shapes: In pool, blindfold one child at a time. For younger children use a wading pool and keep them seated. Put into the pool six to ten sponges cut into easy-to-identify shapes. The shapes can be purchased or cut from regular sponges with scissors. The blindfolded player feels each of the sponges and tries to identify its shape (see photo above). Correct identification wins praise and or a prize. A fish, a plane, a cat, a dog, a duck, a square, a triangle, a circle, and the letters E, S, T, and X are some of the shapes easy to identify.

Sinking the Ship: Take turns seeing how many small rocks, marbles, or plastic toys can be placed on something that floats before it sinks. You might use a plastic boat, a sponge, an aluminum pie plate,

Ping-Pong Ball Race.

or a plastic bowl. If you have identical "ships" and rocks/marbles/toys, more than one child can play at a time.

Ping-Pong Ball Race: Race ping-pong balls across the pool. The players move their balls by using a big spoon or a spatula or an egg beater to stir the water behind the balls (see photo above). No hands may touch the water or balls.

Water Ballet: If you have a large enough pool, hire a swimming teacher to teach the children a water ballet to perform when their parents come to pick them up. Provide life jackets for those who can't swim or are timid in the water.

Raft Stack: Give teams of five or six children identical rafts. See who can most quickly have all of its team members on their raft.

SECTION III

10. Special Things to Eat

When children are together for a party or celebration, they are frequently too excited to eat much. Keep portions small and be ready with second servings for those who want them. Most children prefer familiar, simple foods. Perhaps the best way to provide a sense of "special" food for children is to have something about the food or the manner in which it is served out of the ordinary. With younger children, you may want to put most of your effort into one particular item such as a decorated cake or shaped and decorated cookies. If a food requires a great deal of time, do the preparations ahead of time or substitute something easier.

A helper should assist the person in charge with the last-minute food preparations and with the serving—if possible. Serve drinks after all the children are seated and have their other food.

You may try having someone read a story or play a tape of fun songs while a group of children eats a meal together.

See page 113 for directions on how to make this "boat cake."

Making Foods Different/Attractive: Using the following lists, make faces or decorate the foods in the first list with one or more of the foods on the second list. You might provide the foods and examples and let older children do the decorating before they eat their creation. Be sure the flavors of the items used to decorate complement the food being decorated. For example, raisins would be good for a peanut butter sandwich but olive halves might be a better choice for a grilled cheese sandwich. If they wish, the children can remove the foods used for decorations after they enjoy the appearance, but before eating the food.

Foods to Decorate with Faces or Decorations

sandwiches of all kinds—open face, peanut butter and honey, cream cheese, grilled cheese, deviled ham, lunch meat, cheese
buns—hamburger/hotdog
meat loaves—individual
pizza
scoops of tuna/chicken/egg salad
deviled eggs
macaroni and cheese
baked potatoes mashed and returned to shell

baked potatoes
pancakes
apples/pears/oranges (attach decorations with toothpick pieces)
cakes
cupcakes
cookies and brownies
caramel apples
ice cream balls & cones
ice cream purchased in cups
individual dishes of pudding
jello

Foods to Use to Make Faces or Decorations

olive halves—green or black
pimento
round frankfurter slices
thin strips of carrot, celery, red cabbage, or green, red, or yellow peppers
pickles
grape halves
nuts
small snack foods
raisins
date chunks
green/red cherry halves
coconut—plain or tinted
chocolate chips

butterscotch chips
miniature marshmallows
shaped fruits
small candies—mints, jelly beans, gumdrops, candy kisses, red hots, Life Savers, M&Ms
crushed cookies
graham cracker crumbs
licorice
powdered/brown sugar
colored granulated sugar
icing
whipped topping
baking sprinkles
jams and preserves

Other Food Ideas

- Use ground round beef, crushed cheese-flavored snack crackers, tomato sauce, salt and pepper for quick and tasty individual meat loaves and add olives and pepper or pimento to make faces.
- Pack individual lunches in something different—a plastic sandbox pail, inexpensive toys such as doll beds, trucks, Frisbees—which can be taken home as favors (see photo below). Lunches can also be packed in gift-wrapped boxes.
- Serve doughnuts with a dip of ice cream or sherbet in the center. The ice cream or sherbet may be decorated with a candy face.
- Cut three colors of jello into small cubes, stir the squares into whipped topping and serve in clear plastic cups.
- Use licorice sticks with the ends clipped off as straws for the drink served.
- Freeze Koolaid or juices in freezer trays and serve with a clear soda.
- For a nutritious rabbit face, use two deviled egg halves; split one half lengthwise to use for ears attached to the other half laid yolk side

Refreshments packed in a party favor.

down. Arrange the eggs on lettuce leaves on a platter and add olive slices for eyes and nose and celery strips for whiskers. A slice of cheese can be placed under each rabbit face, if desired.

- Use hollowed hard rolls to make boat sandwiches with chicken, tuna, or egg salad. Attach a paper sail glued to half of a straw or an ice cream stick.
- Bake jelly beans in cupcakes and reward the children who show you the jelly bean in one piece before they eat it.
- Roast wieners and marshmallows on sticks or straightened, unpainted clothes hangers over a campfire. Have a traditional wood fire or substitute a low barbecue grill. Even if an adult does the actual cooking, the child can supervise and enjoy the process. Guard carefully against burns.
- Bake cupcakes in flat-bottomed ice cream cones.
- Make cupcake or muffin piglets using cookies for the snout, candy for the eyes, and adding construction paper ears (see photo below).
- Use shaped cookie cutters to cut bread for open-face sandwiches, lunch meat, cheese slices, or thin jello.
- Combine five cups of crispy rice cereal with a mixture of ¼ cup oleo

Cupcake Piglets.

and 10 ounces of miniature marshmallows melted. To color, add food coloring to the oleo and marshmallows. Cut into shapes; the colored shapes will make a pretty tray of snacks.

- Bake two identical pie crust shapes with jam in the middle and the top sprinkled with colored granulated sugar.
- Soften ice cream and shape into paper liners in cupcake pans, decorate, and freeze.
- Roll ice cream balls in coconut tinted with food coloring, chopped nuts, or baking sprinkles.
- Add brown cookie ears and candy eyes and nose to a scoop of chocolate ice cream to make a bear face. Keep in the freezer until time to serve.
- Place pointed ice cream cones on top of ice cream balls and put a face on the ice cream with candies or frosting to create a clown with a hat.
- A large marshmallow in the bottom of an ice cream cone will provide a surprise treat and help prevent leaking of the ice cream.
- Top party-size round breads with a mixture of 1 pound of cooked and drained sausage, 1 pound of melted Velveeta cheese, ½ cup of ketchup, 1 teaspoon of oregano, and ½ teaspoon of garlic powder. Bake these miniature pizzas at 350 degrees about 10 minutes. They may be fixed ahead of time and frozen until party time.

Decorated Cakes to Feature

Decorated cakes are almost a necessity for a birthday party and a favorite of children any time. If you wish to do your own decorating, consider the following ideas:

- Tint white cake batter and or icing to complement your decorating scheme.
- Create letters for names, numbers for age, and or borders with baking sprinkles, chocolate chips, gumdrops, M&Ms, red and green cherries, or other small edible items.
- Purchase and use a set of reusable plastic letters and numbers designed for bulletin boards. Check a school supply store for these.
- Use pastel mint wafers to create flowers or balloons with licorice string stems and leaves or balloon strings.
- Cookie cutters are good for making shape patterns on cake icing which can be filled in with colored icing from tubes.

- Animal crackers or plastic animals make a fun "zoo" cake. Cover the top of the cake with green tinted coconut before you set the animals in place.
- Hold a purchased or homemade stencil in a desired shape over a cake and sift powdered or colored granulated sugar through the stencil onto the cake icing.
- Plastic flowers around the base of a cake or decorating the top can be removed after the cake is admired and before the pieces are cut.
- Small flags and sparklers add zest to a July 4 cake.
- Large marshmallows can be used as holders for candles and decorations.
- Check the toy departments for collections of miniature plastic people and animals. You can often find just what you need for cakes featuring cowboys, farm animals, superheroes, dollhouse-type families and furniture, and the like.
- Laminate paper dolls or pictures or designs made of paper or light cardboard and use them to decorate a cake. If they need to stand up, attach them to coffee stirrers, straws or Popsicle/ice cream sticks. Many school supply stores laminate materials and charge by the foot.
- Decorate round cake layers to look like the faces of kids (see photo below). Use tinted coconut, shaved chocolate candy bars, or colored icing to form the hair. Black licorice makes good eyebrows, nose, and mouth. Small candies make eyes, lips, and hair ribbons. Check the list of foods to use for decorating on page 108 for more ideas. You might call your faces "Kake Kids" or give them names.

"Kake Kids."

- A round cake lends itself to creating a clock with the hands pointing to a special time — a time of birth, the time of the party, or the time school begins, for example.
- Make a round basketball cake with orange icing and black licorice to create seam lines. Use white icing and red laces for a baseball team or World Series party cake.
- A round cake makes a pumpkin cake for Thanksgiving or a jack-o-lantern cake for Halloween.
- Stack two round cakes; ice the top with white and the top edge and sides with a bright color. Place flat suckers around the edge, slanted with the tops alternating to give the look of a drum. Stick two suckers in the top to represent drum sticks.

My favorite "special" cakes are those cut into interesting shapes and decorated. The following are some suggestions for you to try.

BUNNY from 2 round (8 or 9 inch) cakes: Split the cake which will become the ears in half. Position it on your platter or cake board the way you want the ears to lay (see placement guide at left) and then trim the bottoms so they will lay flat with the cut edges close to the cake.

The cake in the photo on page 114 has white icing with coconut. The insides of the ears are peach colored icing and the features are formed from candy and licorice strips. This is an easy, but delightful dessert and especially appropriate for Easter gatherings.

BOAT from a 9×13 inch cake: The sails probably should be covered with white icing, but the rest of the decoration of the boat can reflect your color scheme. Here is one example of a color scheme: white sails, red sour balls down the center of the sails, a brown hull with yellow icing and sour ball life preservers, and jelly bean people. The A on the sail in the illustration on page 107 may be substituted with the

Bunny cake.

initial of your family's last name. The initial and the ropes down the center of the sails may be made of red licorice. A cutting and placement guide is shown on page 115.

VAN *from a 9 × 13 inch cake:* The van in the photo on page 116 is blue, because we own a blue van. Black licorice creates the lines, marshmallow pies cut in half were substituted for the cake tires in the design, pink jelly beans represent passengers, yellow jelly beans make the headlights, and a black jelly bean serves as the hood ornament. A cutting and placement guide is shown on page 116.

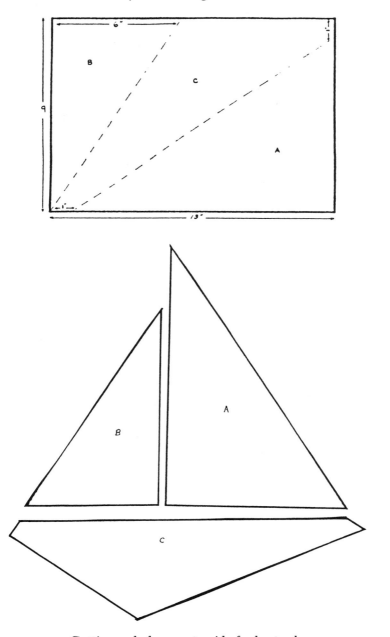

Cutting and placement guide for boat cake.

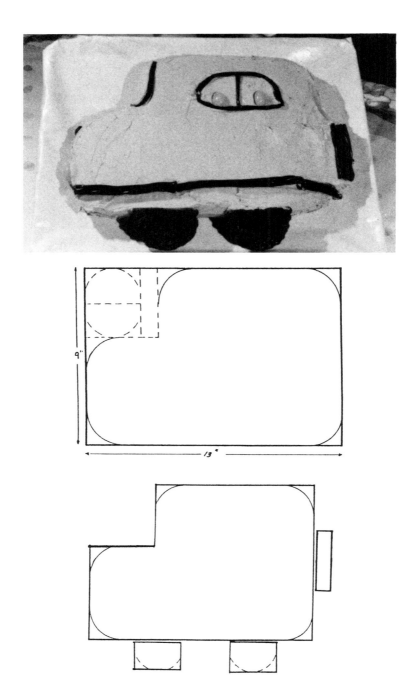

Top: Van cake; *bottom:* Cutting and placement guides for van cake.

SANTA *from an 8 inch square and an 8 inch round cake:* Make Santa's beard and hat band and hat tassel from white icing and coconut. Ice his hat with red icing and his face with pink icing. Use candies for his eyes, nose, cheeks and mouth (see photo on page 118). A cutting and placement guide is shown below.

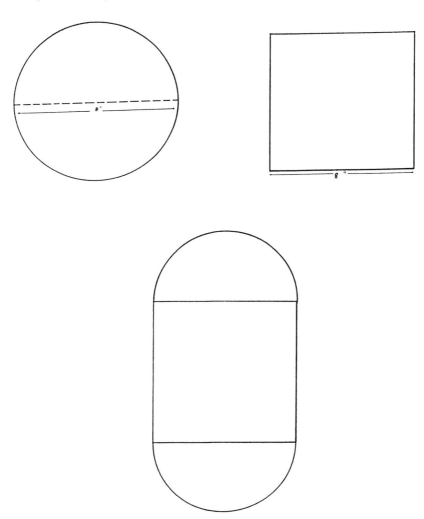

Cutting and placement guide for Santa cake.

Santa cake.

BOOTS/CHRISTMAS STOCKING *from a 9×13 inch cake:* A few quick cuts can turn a cake into two boots or Christmas stockings (see cutting guide on page 119). A heavy batter cake, rather than a light one, will work best for this cake because of the long cut edges to be iced. The cake in the photo on page 119 is iced in bright green with a white and coconut band at the top. The loops at the tops are made of pipe cleaners. The letters spelling the names are plastic letters made for bulletin boards.

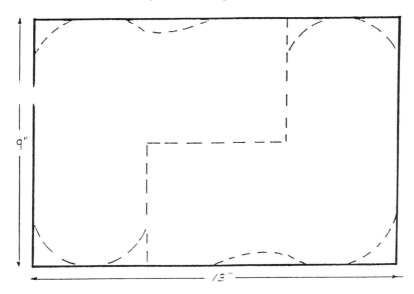

Cutting guide for boots/Christmas stocking cake.

Christmas stocking cake.

Lion cake.

LION from a 10 inch round cake: This cake requires a construc-tion paper or posterboard shape to provide the illusion of a mane. Use gold colored construction paper and yellow cake icing. Form the mouth with icing or licorice, use candy for features, and position two fortune cookies as ears (see photo above).

TRAIN from two loaf cakes: A whole loaf cake creates the engine. A cookie stack, a spool of thread, or a film container will make a smoke stack. Split the other loaf cake to create two cars of different heights. Use half cookies or round candies for wheels and licorice to form win-dows and doors. Animal crackers or plastic cars can ride on the train cars (see photo on page 121).

Helpful Hints for Decorating Cakes

- For easy to remove cakes, line pans with wax paper after applying a coat of vegetable oil.
- Place wax paper under the sides of the cake while frosting to keep the platter or cake board clean.

Train cake.

- When doing a shaped cake—make a pattern of the shape out of paper and use the paper as a cutting guide.
- If the cut edges of a cake are difficult to ice, glaze them with a mixture of confectionary sugar and milk.

Special Occasion Foods for Children

The following is a list of foods to consider preparing for children on special occasions. Keep in mind that the all-time favorites are the familiar hamburgers, hotdogs, pizza, macaroni and cheese, decorated cakes, cookies and ice cream.

- hamburgers
- hotdogs
- hotdogs baked in cresent roll or refrigerator biscuit dough—with or without cheese
- pizza
- individual meat loaf
- grilled cheese sandwiches
- bite-size fried chicken
- peanut butter and jelly or honey sandwiches
- cream cheese on dollar rolls or shaped bread for open sandwiches
- assorted cold cut and cheese sandwiches on buns
- pita bread roll-up sandwich—secured with toothpicks
- macaroni and cheese

- assorted bite-size foods—perhaps on a party toothpick—small canned Vienna sausages, frankfurter slices, meatballs, ham cubes, cheese cubes, grapes, apple slices, pieces of bologna and cream cheese roll, melon cubes
- raw vegetable pieces to dip in sour cream base dips and or peanut butter
- deviled eggs
- fruit slices or pieces
- French toast sprinkled with sifted powdered sugar applied through a stencil
- pancakes—chocolate chip faces, powdered sugar designs or fruit toppings
- big soft pretzels
- popcorn—plain or flavored
- popcorn balls—held together with caramel mix or canned cake icing
- mixes—mix together three or more of foods like pretzel pieces, nuts, cereals toasted in butter and salt, chow mein noodles, raisins, date pieces, M&Ms, gumdrops, or jelly beans. (These mixes may be rejected by some of the children but loved by others.)
- nuts in the shell—supervise the cracking and picking out
- chow mein noodles
- snack crackers, pretzels, chips, and cheese balls—consider individual bags
- taco chips—with or without hot cheese topping
- cake (see special section beginning on page 111 for decorated and cut-up cakes)
- cupcakes
- muffins
- sweet bread slices (pumpkin, banana, nut, carrot)
- cookies
- fortune cookies
- ice cream—offer one kind, or two at the most—best choices are probably vanilla, chocolate, or Neapolitan
- ice cream balls—decorated
- ice cream cones
- sherbet
- milk shakes
- ice cream sundaes
- ice cream sodas
- snow cones
- frozen fruit juice sticks

- pudding
- jello
- hot fudge, caramel sauce, or fruit ice cream toppings over cake, cup-cakes, muffins, fruit, or ice cream
- chocolate drop candies, smashed and eaten between crackers
- doughnuts
- juices/punch in individual boxes with a straw — offers convenience and reduces spills
- lemonade and frozen strawberry punch
- sherbet and clear soda punch
- Koolaid mixed with soda of same color/flavor
- milk — add food coloring and perhaps a little flavoring
- hot chocolate
- warm apple juice or cider with cinnamon added

11. Favors and Prizes

Favors are small gifts or decorative items given to all the guests at a party. Prizes are given as a reward to winners.

Favors

Favors, even simple and inexpensive ones, are very appreciated by children. Handing out party bags (see some ideas below) or packaged favors at the end of the party is a nice way to say good-bye. The birthday child may pass out favors just after the opening of birthday gifts.

Party Bags: A party bag for each child can be made by using lunch bags, gift bags, grocery bags, large baggies, small trash bags, large socks, or cloth bags sewn from fabric. The bags may be decorated to complement the theme of a party. The single most important requirement for the party bag is that it be labeled with a child's name (see illustration at right).

Prizes

Consider nonmaterial rewards for young children who win, instead of prizes. Suggested rewards for winning:

- taking a bow to cheering and clapping
- going first in the next game

- sitting in a special chair
- receiving a ribbon award, attached by a safety pin
- having a fun sticker attached to the shoulder

Prizes for winners seem to become more important to children after they reach the first grade. If you do give prizes, be sure everyone goes home with at least one. Have a game in which all win a prize or have creative categories for winning such as trying hardest, the best sport, or helping with the game. Very inexpensive prizes such as candy, gum, balloons, and packages of fruits can be placed on a tray and winners can select one item when they win. More expensive prizes should be labeled with names as they are won and or placed in a party bag marked with the child's name. A teenage or adult helper may be needed for this task.

List of Ideas for Favors and Prizes

activity book
animal crackers
animal sponges
balloons
balls
barrettes
beanbags
billfold
book
book for telephone numbers
box of paper stars
bracelet
bubble blower and liquid
button
candy
card games
change purse
colored index cards
coloring book
comb
comic book
compass
cookies
cookies, shaped or decorated
  (bakery or homemade)
craft project
crayons

cup
diary
fancy erasers
fancy paper clips
fancy pencil sharpeners
fancy plastic straws
fancy shoelaces
fashion doll
flashlight
Frisbee
game
glass
gum
hats/caps/scarves
headband
hero doll
instant photograph
jacks
jump rope
kaleidoscope
key chain
kite
Life Savers/mint candies
lollipop
children's magazine
magic slate
magnet

magnifying glasses
marbles
markers
miniature plastic people or animals
mirror
modeling clay
necklace
notebook
paddle ball
pail and shovel
paper dolls
paperback joke book
pencil/school box
pencils
pens
plants
plastic car games

puzzles
ribbon
ring
sample bubble bath
shaped notebooks
small airplane/car/truck
small doll
small purse
small stuffed animal
snack food—individual packages
sports cards
stencils
stickers
water pistol
whistle
yo-yo

General Suggestions

- Favors can serve as decorations, game props, refreshment place cards, or refreshment containers during the party and then go home with the children.
- Have favors and prizes relate to the party theme.
- A teacher can usually order inexpensive paperback books for you.
- Buy packages of small toys or candy and divide them.
- Carnival supply stores or catalogs will have many things you need at good prices.
- Craft stores are good sources of prizes and favors.
- Buy at special sales and at discount and dollar stores.
- Consult a child about what the other children will like.
- Preparing and making favors for a party can provide great entertainment for one or two children.

12. Decorating Ideas

- Consider having the child in your home or a neighbor child help make the party decorations. A best friend might also be included in the projects. Sometimes a teenager will delight in taking over the project if you supply the pattern and materials.
- Keep party decorations for younger children simple. Decorations become more important to children when they reach nine to ten years of age.
- Decorated place mats and napkin rings made of construction or other heavy papers make the table pretty, can contribute to the theme, and make clean-up easier. You might select black and orange for Halloween, red and green for Christmas, and a color to coordinate with the trim of the cake for a birthday. Decorate the place mats and napkin rings with things such as bought stickers, glue and glitter borders, cartoon characters from the comic strips, stick figure children drawn with a marker, each child's name, and a flower design. If you put a great deal of work into the place mats, consider having them laminated at a school supply story so they can become favors or be saved to use again. A decorated cake or other centerpiece adds to the attractiveness of the table, but do not use anything so tall the children cannot see over and around it.
- Arrange favors in a pretty basket or a big bowl until distributed.
- It is a good idea to provide pin-on name tags and name place-setting cards at the refreshment table. Both of these items should support the color scheme and the party theme.
- Make a life-size scarecrow, hobo, snowman, clown, witch, ghost, Santa, or other large figure by stuffing clothes with newspaper balls (see photo on page 128). Seat the figure in a chair. Use safety pins, elastic, masking tape, and other appropriate means of attaching the parts to each other and to the chair. I like to use the large figures to mark the party house and be part of the welcome the guests receive. They can also be the center of attraction for a photo session.

Life-Size Figure.

- Dress up stuffed animals and or dolls to complement the color scheme and or theme.
- Scatter confetti on bushes and trees or on sidewalks in front of the house just before the party.
- Put a welcoming banner over the front door or the door to the party area.
- Secure a small tree, remove the leaves, and fit it in a stand. Use Christmas ornament hangers and decorate it with appropriate

shapes, gumdrops, small plastic toys, or some shape or item related to the party theme.

- Helium balloons can be used in many ways; if you have one per child — and a few spares — send them home as treasured favors. Let the helium balloons float at the ceiling in the play area. Write names on them and anchor them with a metal washer at each child's place to eat. Use a cluster of balloons to form a centerpiece at the table.
- Regular balloons will cling to walls if you rub them against your clothes or hair to create static electricity. Tie clusters of balloons on the mailbox or porch to mark the party house (see illustration at left).
- Use aluminum foil or gold florist foil to cover cardboard shapes or to form fantasy animals to use in a mobile.
- Crepe paper streamers can make canopies, form bows, hang in strips in doorways, be twisted around porch posts, or rope off play areas. Streamers can be attached to walls and ceilings with dabs of toothpaste which will wash off easily after the party.
- Bought or home-made posters can often be the focal point of a theme.
- Make a piñata by decorating a brown sack, filling it with candy, and hanging it by a strong cord until time for the bursting activity which will give the children the candy and toys inside.
- Use coat hangers to make mobiles with small toys, pretty shapes, or plastic flowers. Hang the items at different lengths and hang the mobiles from light fixtures and in doorways.
- Make or buy party hats. A carnival supply store is an excellent source of inexpensive hats. An even less expensive alternative is making your own from construction paper. Look for plain cone-shaped party hats to decorate with stickers and or bows. Bandannas, wide ribbons, and colorful cloth strips can be tied around heads as sweatbands and decorated with buttons, glitter, small balloons, and feathers.

- Write the children's names on their paper cups or place mats with glue and glitter.
- Buy solid color vinyl place mats and decorate them with permanent-ink markers.
- Add stickers, appropriate to the theme, to colored napkins.
- Consider colored sheets for tablecloths.
- Attach decorations to the table with double-stick tape or masking tape rolled to make it double stick; this will keep items in place — at least for a while.

Appendix: Gift Suggestions

This list is for when you don't know the child well and have no favorite gift idea of your own for the age level needed.

Gift suggestions are provided for each age — 3 to 10 years old — and for four price ranges. You should consider the suggestions on all four sides of the category you are interested in, because the age level and price ranges overlap.

	Estimated Price Range	
Age	*Under $3*	*$4 to $6*
3	flash light tub toy dish set	wooden puzzle Play Doh plastic animals
4	ball squirt gun play jewelry set	Nerf ball & hoop padlock and key doctor's kit
5	coloring book & crayons small cowboys & Indians paper dolls	play tea set word flash cards Cootie game
6	baseball cards small car set puzzle	ring toss game necklace garden digging tool
7	magnets sunglasses magnifying glass	Blockhead game pail and shovel Barrel of Monkeys
8	art supplies Chinese checkers comic books	poster pencil case mini sports ball
9	card game hole punch Sowish ball	compass mystery story book wireless microphone
10	scrapbook bubble bath shaped note pads	poster Nerf football cork bulletin board and push pins

	Estimated Price Range	
Age	*$7 to $10*	*$11 to $15*
3	stuffed animal	play telephone
	wooden blocks	learn to dress doll
	fire engine	jack-in-the-box
4	fashion doll/clothes	nursery school blocks
	picture lotto game	Magna-Doodle
	ironing board set	dump truck
5	animal dominoes	purse
	Candyland game	watch
	baby doll with bottle	doll carriage
6	U.S.A. puzzle map	Nerf bat & ball
	colorful umbrella	lunch box
	stencil shapes set	Tinker Toys
7	puppet	Monopoly Junior
	chalk and chalkboard	school bag
	beach towel	stapler
8	Operation game	Nerf Ping-Pong
	bulletin board	overnight suitcase
	sing-along tape & song-book	cassette player
9	kite	label punch & tape
	decorated T–shirt	slumber bag
	pocket calculator	Twister game
10	Frisbee	craft kit
	Skip-Bo Cards	basketball
	Mille Bornes cards	Scrabble

Index

133

Index